S L A N T S I X

New Theater from Minnesota's Playwrights' Center

Edited by
Morgan Jenness,
John Richardson,
& Mac Wellman

NEW RIVERS PRESS
1990

Slant/Six has been published with the aid of grants from the McKnight Foundation (a Partnership in the Arts Award administered by the Metropolitan Regional Arts Council), the Arts Development Fund of the United Arts Council, the First Bank System Foundation, Liberty State Bank, the Tennant Company Foundation, the Valspar Corporation, the Star Tribune/Cowles Media Company, the Elizabeth A. Hale Fund of the Minneapolis Foundation, and the National Endowment for the Arts (with funds appropriated by the Congress of the United States).

New Rivers Press wants to express special thanks to Katherine R. Maehr, our Managing Editor, who nurtured *Slant/Six* through its long and often difficult journey to our printer, and to Caroline Garrett Taber (our cover artist), who has the patience of an elephant and the lightness of a gazelle.

New Rivers Press books are distributed by

The Talman Company	Bookslinger
150-5th Avenue	502 North Prior Avenue
New York, NY 10011	St. Paul, MN 55104

Slant/Six has been manufactured in the United States of America for New Rivers Press (C. W. Truesdale, Editor/Publisher), 420 North 5th St., Suite 910, Minneapolis, MN 55401 and for the Playwrights' Center (David Moore, Jr., Executive Director), 2301 Franklin Avenue East, Minneapolis, MN 55406, in a first edition of 2,000 copies.

For C. G. T.
And For Steve Goodwin
of the National Endowment for the Arts

CONTENTS

Introduction

ONE OF THE cultural riches of this country is the multiplicity of viewpoints which it encompasses. One of the vital strengths of the Playwrights' Center is how it has reflected that multiplicity through the spectrum of writers and writings it has supported—most notably writers such as Lee Blessing, Ping Chong, Barbara Field, and August Wilson.

Though hardly pretending to reflect the entire demographic field that exists, the plays in this volume were chosen not only for their strong and distinctive writing but because they all examine the world and society from diverse and perhaps less familiar angles. The plays all seem to deal with various different individuals' struggles to place themselves in context, to locate themselves within the geography of their own worlds and society at large.

William S. Yellow Robe, Jr.'s play *Sneaky*, shows us how members of the virtually annihilated original culture of this country strike a blow to maintain a continuance of the culture in their insistence on observing the ritual of death in their own traditional way. The sons who steal their mother's body, believing the white cultural burial will trap her soul, reidentify themselves with their "illegal" action and form a stronger bond among themselves. "That's the way we've always done things—by ourselves and together."

In Martha Boesing's *The Business at Hand*, a pair of friends once identified by their political activism come to terms with changes in each other, themselves and the temper of the times. Although they face hard truths, they also emerge from the encounter with a potentially clearer picture of how they fit into and wish to affect their world, as well as a deeper understanding of what may motivate their desires. "It isn't the earth we want to save, or the victims of our foreign policies, or even the Eileens or the wounded birds—it is ourselves."

Growing Up Queer in America is indeed the primary focus of Chris Cinque's play, which also reveals startling images of Santa Claus, first love, Catholicism and New Jersey. A young woman traces the evolution of her identity as a lesbian in a morally-repressed society as parallel to Dante's *Divine Comedy*, as she journeys from the hell of guilt and doubt to the paradise of ecstasy and self-acceptance and fulfills "the role of queers since time immemorial, that of oracle and guide."

Though seeming to deal with a more traditional, small town Midwest family, Patrick Smith's *Driving Around the House* reveals cracks and fissures in the desired Rockwell portrait of the American family. A young man cuts through time, space and memory to reinvestigate the childhood oc-curences and the painful familial relationships, secrets, betrayals and deser-tions which marked his place on an insecure terrain. "Her high heels clicked on the sidewalk and she said they still loved each other but they made each other sad and they needed to be apart. I listened to the road and wondered where we were."

Though perhaps included more for the extraordinarily strong rhythmic and linguistic choices in T.J. Lappin's writing, *Hit By a Cab* also echoes the attempt to mark one's place in a tenuous landscape. The shadowy characters of the play's 1949 world could easily transfer to the present time in their longing to find a way out of their limbos, as they literally and figuratively attempt merely to cross a street without being run over by the kinetic mechanism of a world which often seems impenetrable. "Fix their eyes to the ends of long wires, and from the balcony lift up their eyelids slowly."

Judy McGuire's solo character in one of her *Interview* pieces surrounds herself with maps and charts, longitude and latitude, geological history of the planet, and the art of the paper copier, combined with the precise, prosaic, and profound personal details in order to help locate her, for us and herself, in the geography of her life. "You probably don't recognize me away from the Sharp Bond Paper Copier, but you're going to enjoy meeting the woman behind the machine."

This volume is therefore a first attempt to capture some of the rich and diverse voices which have emanated from the Playwrights' Center. It is the first attempt to represent a varied group who share the ability to observe and reveal to us the world in which we live, from another angle, with a different slant—*Slant/Six*.

— *Morgan Jenness*

IT IS NOT BIG news to observe that plays are meant to be performed on the stage in front of audiences, and exist as an entirely different class of objects when published in an anthology, as initiates to the hallowed status of dramatic literature. Some go so far as to say that the "play" exists only in performance—that the playscript is but a conventional and inadequate transcription of an outline for performance.

Most new playscripts subscribe to a familiar and readily accessible per-formance strategy. Since I have seen many plays on the stage, I can easily imagine these new playscripts in performance. Their beginnings, middles and endings behave just like the same portions of the playscripts I studied in college as dramatic literature. The story of the play comes out of the mouths of the characters in a familiar fashion. The characters function as discrete units, comfortably resembling the constructs I carry in my head for how literary personalities are allowed to behave. In short I can read the playscript and decipher the performance strategy without feeling excluded from the essential elements of performance.

Not all new playscripts readily give out their performance strategy. And if I read them wielding my cultural bias toward dramatic literature I will get a headache and think them "bad" plays for not conforming to my accumulated notion of how plays ought behave. As an avid reader of new playscripts I must remind myself to read also between the lines of the text, to try to capture the often unfamiliar performance strategy. These playscripts I must try to read on their own terms. They may not flatter and tickle my accepted notions of dramatic construction. They may intentionally misbehave with secret stories that exclude me from the performance and characters who refute my concepts of organic personality. They may, in fact, if I read them carefully enough, add to and enrich my notions of dramatic literature.

Each of the six playscripts in this anthology has its own slant on performance. My initial experience has not been through reading, but through some manner of performance. Reading them in the context of this anthology leads me to remember the pleasure and richness of performance that all too often evaporates in the dry act of reading.

When Chris Cinque performs her monologue, *Growing Up Queer in America*, holding in public view quoted materials from Dante and the courageous reportage of her most personal experiences, her presence onstage adds force to the associations that arise from the juxtaposition of these materials. It is her presence in performance that gives me vision.

In Judy McGuire's *Interview* pieces, the inspection of the commonplace is magnified by the irony of performance. Can you find the affectless slapstick from merely reading? But look in a mirror and recite "Mary Worth," etc., and something begins to happen that the page can't capture.

Patrick Smith's *Driving Around the House* offers an example of a performance strategy that doesn't reveal itself to the casual reader. One of the main actions of this play, Grownup Paddy's voyeurism, is carried forward without great affect. Grownup Paddy is constantly watching the events that made up his life, but the play allows him only a flat affectless narrator's introduction. The emotionality of his watching is hidden from the reader, but in constant view of the theatre audience during performance. As you read this play imagine the unspoken anger, bitterness, and affection that might rise up and be repressed by the watching Grownup Paddy, and you will discover the key to the play's dramatic heart.

In Terry Lappin's *Hit By A Cab* don't be put off by the mystifying absence of event. This play refuses to tell its story other than in the music of its language. The rhythms of the dialogue are the rhythms of exhausted passion and spent opportunity. The entire play proceeds as if the main events of life have already passed. The play assumes we know all this and eschews exposition as it speaks directly to us in confidence. It assumes we know that Mr. Udey is dying of an infected tattoo. It assumes we know that Harry is a stubbornly talentless stand-up comic, a fool for a bitterly humorless world. It is a world of failed feeling, and the play assumes we will recognize ourselves without extraneous cues. It does not exclude its audience by distancing it with explanations.

All of these plays aggressively take the stage. Each has its own rules for performance. So read slowly, dreamily, and imagine how to fill a space with the words of these writers.

— *John Richardson*

A VERY SHORT six-cleft somewhat spreading limb; the sixx-legg'd nation in the fields appear; hail candle-light! an imaginary general illumination consisting of verybright short sixes; lat nat this wrechched wo thyn herte gnawe, But manly set the world on sexe and seuen; I have never knows the children. It's just six of one half-a-dozen of the other; like little boys & girls who wore their hair in "number sixes" at the temples, when law had left them hair sufficient for such ornamentation; six drachms of barbadoes aloes, six ounces of Epsom salts.

— *Mac Wellman*

WHEN I STEP BACK from the dozens of projects currently underway at the Playwrights' Center, I observe that these playwrights, as a group, are exploring a range of subjects and forms fully as diverse as that of the American theater itself. I am hard put to conceive of one anthology that might somehow represent them all. Nor does this book try, but seeks instead to assemble a particular body of visions and experience—a particular arrangement of theatrical "slants."

Four of the playwrights selected live in Minnesota, one in New York, and one recently has moved from Missoula, Montana to Seattle, Washington. Each has or has had her/his own way of working with the Play-wrights' Center, particular to the imagination and nature of each of their writing. All work in other areas of the theater, too: several of them direct or act, and one is currently a literary manager. All of them write for a theater that wants to effect change in some realm, whether in individual consciousness, our grasp of history or our place in culture.

Many deserve credit for this book. Bill Truesdale first proposed it, and, with valuable assistance from Katherine Maehr and John Minczeski has given it the same tender care that all New Rivers Press publications receive.

Morgan Jenness, John Richardson and Mac Wellman have understood the selection of these plays to be a matter not of competition but their own editorial judgment. They have approached this work with personal investment and the hope that their decisions, made together, might make a difference to our contemporary theater's evolving repertory.

Others were generous with their technical advice: John Del Vecchio, Kip Gould of Broadway Play Publishing, Diane Lamar, Jim Leverett and Terence Nemeth at Theatre Communications Group, David E. LeVine of the Dramatists Guild, Susan Schulman, and Philip Dean Stoller of the Authors Guild.

Certainly this book would not be possible without the generous sup-port from the McKnight Foundation and its Partnership in the Arts Award (administered by the Metropolitan Regional Arts Council) we received in 1988.

Deepest thanks of all go to the six playwrights participating in this pro-ject: Martha Boesing, Chris Cinque, Terrance J. Lappin, Judy McGuire, Patrick Smith and William S. Yellow Robe, Jr. It is for these writers and their colleagues that the Playwrights' Center exists.

— *David Moore, Jr.*
Executive Director
The Playwrights' Center

SLANT/SIX IS THE product of a dream we at New Rivers have long had—of doing a series of drama anthologies, the only area of contemporary literature not previously covered by our other programs.

In the spring of 1988 we applied for and received a McKnight Partnership in the Arts grant to do just such an anthology in cooperation with the Playwrights' Center in Minneapolis. The P. C. has long been recognized as a major force for new theater all over the country, but this is the first time it has been directly involved with the publication of new plays. New

Rivers has been publishing contemporary poetry, fiction, translations, and personal essays for nearly 25 years and is recognized throughout America and in other countries as well as a bold and innovative publisher of new writing. So, this is a natural partnership, a marriage of like minds from very different backgrounds.

The competition that the Playwrights' Center and New Rivers set up was modeled to a certain extent on our successful and highly respected Minnesota Voices Project (an annual competition for new and emerging authors of poetry, fiction, and personal essays). Each year the four or five MVP winning book-length manuscripts are selected by a panel of five professional writers and editors. In the case of *Slant/Six*, we set up a three-judge panel, two of whom (Morgan Jenness and John Richardson) were selected by the Playwrights' Center and the third (Mac Wellman) by New Rivers. David Moore, Jr. and I served as *ad hoc*, non-voting members of that panel. The panel met in the spring of 1989 and worked its way through around 25 finalist plays of extraordinary variety and strength—all by Core or Alumni Members of the P.C. The sessions were intense, stormy, exciting, good-humored, and provocative—the way any really good panel should be. Each of the three judges has strong personal preferences—and no two lists were anything like the same. The result—like all New Rivers anthologies—is a collection that is diverse in character and voice, and profoundly original. We are proud to put our imprint on this book and to have it join the company of first-rate books and anthologies we have published over the years.

Slant/Six grew out of our conviction (shared by the people at the Playwrights' Center) that good plays are not only performable but *readable*. Reading plays, however (which I love to do), requires a slightly different sort of imagination of the reader—something like what happens when you listen to old-time radio plays but not quite, because you have to supply not only the bodies and the scenes but the voices too. You need to *hear* the voices in these plays, just as you need to *hear* poetry before you try to get it with your mind. Perhaps the best thing is to sound out some of these lines and scenes. Then, if you have an opportunity to go to a production of one of them, you can compare your version with what you see on the boards and maybe even get some pleasure out of the differences.

I have one other little story to tell you and that's about how we came up with the title for the book. After the panel had chosen the six playwrights included here, we were all sitting around drinking wine and beer and brainstorming about the title. We wanted to come up with something that suggested that all these playwrights were, in one way or another, "off-center," had points of view outside of the mainstream. I am not generally an advocate of the kind of brain-storming that goes on in ad agencies, but I do have to admit it really worked on that hot spring day. Morgan and I came up with the word "slant" and then the fact that Patrick Smith's play is called *Driving Around the House* and is set in 1963 brought to my mind the fact that the Chrysler Corporation's great engine of that time—the one that powered the Dodge Dart and Charger and Plymouth Valiant—was called the "slant-six." Only a slight leap brought to mind that there are *six* playwrights represented here. Everyone was happy.

And we at New Rivers are very happy too, to be able to bring you this fine collection of plays.

— *C. W. Truesdale*
Editor/Publisher
New Rivers Press

MARTHA BOESING

The Business at Hand

MARTHA BOESING was the Founder, Artistic Director and Playwright-in-Residence from 1974-1984 of Minneapolis' At the Foot of the Mountain, the oldest, continuously producing, professional women's theater in America. She was a core member of the Firehouse Theater Company in Minneapolis from 1964-68, librettist for the Minnesota Opera Company in 1969-70, playwright-in-residence at the Academy Theater in Atlanta from 1972-1974, core member of the Playwrights' Center (1983-1987), and the writer/director for both In the Heart of the Beast Puppet and Mask Theater of Minneapolis (1986 and 1989) and for San Francisco's A Traveling Jewish Theatre (1988-1989).

She began her thirty-seven year theater career—which includes performing, directing, playwrighting, administering, designing and doing odd jobs—as an apprentice in summer stock when she was sixteen. Two college degrees and three children later, Martha has authored more than thirty scripts and librettos all of which have been produced throughout the country and in Canada, Great Britain, Germany and Australia, and nine of which have been published. Over the years she has given lectures, taught classes in playwriting and acting, led countless workshops, and been the subject of essays, articles and books relating to her work as a leading feminist theater artist in this country. She has spent her career on the cutting edge of the American theater movement, creating and directing plays which have a radical voice and an iconoclastic aesthetic.

She resides in Minneapolis and is currently at work on two new plays and a book about environmental activism.

THE BUSINESS AT HAND was commissioned by the Playwrights' Center for the Jones one-act play award in 1987. The play was workshopped in May of 1987 with Buffy Sedlachek and Paul Boesing as Mimi and Sol, and D. Scott Glasser directing. Originally the play did not incorporate the stage directions in the text, but I began adding a few of them, and as we workshopped the piece I became more and more intrigued with the manipulation of mood the stage directions afforded the inner life of the characters. Read out loud, they became an expression of the subtextual and more universal dance which was going on between them, about control and surrender, sexuality, the fear of intimacy, and ultimately —when she breaks the rules by saying what she is really feeling— about the breakdown of communication between men and women (even radical men and women) in this white, male-dominated society.

The Business at Hand was first produced at the Actors Theatre in St. Paul as part of the 1988 Minnesota One-Act Play Festival, directed by D. Scott Glasser with Claudia Wilkens playing Mimi and David Lenthall playing Sol.

— *Martha Boesing*

There are two characters: A woman (Mimi) and a man (Sol). The play takes place in Mimi's apartment or on an empty stage with a few rehearsal props.

MIMI: (*Moving around the apartment*) Mimi, an actress, aged, pause . . . forty nine, walks around her tastefully decorated apartment on the top floor of an old estate in a northern American city. She checks the fire, she moves one of the chairs closer to another, she crosses up to the garret window which looks out over the city. It is snowing outside. She wonders if he's changed. Does he still eat meat? She checks the time. She decides to change her clothes. She heads for the bedroom. (*She does so.*)

SOL: (*He knocks at the door.*) Sol waits. (*Shifts his weight.*) He shifts his weight from one foot to the other. (*He knocks again.*)

MIMI: There is a knock at the door. Mimi crosses to the door. (*She does so.*) She checks her make-up in the mirror. (*She does so.*)

SOL: Sol waits, breathes.

MIMI: She opens the door. (*She does so.*) Sol stands in the corridor, dressed in khaki pants, an old sweater, coat, boots and his inimitable baseball cap.

SOL: He looks at her.

MIMI: She looks at him.

SOL: Hi! (*He brushes the snow off and removes his coat.*)

MIMI: Well, hello! He brushes off the snow and removes his coat. He's early. You're early.

SOL: Am I? (*He checks his watch.*)

MIMI: He checks his watch. He laughs.

SOL: (*He laughs.*) I guess I am. It's a habit of mine. Its because I'm ahead of the times! (*Mimi laughs.*) She laughs.

MIMI: Pause.

SOL: She invites him in.

MIMI: Well, come on in! (*He does so.*)

SOL: Thanks. She notices his dirty boots on her clean floor. He removes them and leaves them by the door. (*He does so.*)

MIMI: He looks good. You look terrific — how about a real greeting?

SOL: She opens her arms. (*They hug.*) God, it's good to be out!

MIMI: I bet. How was it? He doesn't know how to answer. Wait. Don't say a word. Sit down. I'll get you a drink. (*She exits.*)

SOL: Mimi goes to the kitchen.

MIMI: She returns. (*She does so.*) She notices he is still standing. Whiskey, isn't it? Straight up?

SOL: With a little ice. It was hell.

MIMI: Of course. (*She exits.*)

SOL: Boring, lonely, and smelly.

MIMI: (*She enters with the drinks.*) Don't they clean the cells?

SOL: Constantly. Smells like a hospital. (*Mimi laughs.*) She laughs. (*Sol laughs. She gives him his drink.*)

MIMI: He laughs. (*She raises her glass.*)

SOL: She's lifting her glass.

MIMI: To your homecoming. I'm glad to have you back, Sol.

SOL: Thanks. (*He drinks.*)

MIMI: He drinks. (*She looks at him.*)

SOL: She looks at him over the rim of her glass. Ah, wonderful!

MIMI: He smiles. . .a lot. (*She sits.*)

SOL: She sits.

MIMI: He sits. (*He does so.*)

(*Sol lights a cigarette, looks around for an ashtray, as she speaks.*)

MIMI: He lights up a cigarette and looks around for an ashtray. She fetches one for him from the mantlepiece (*Does so.*), and then sits again. (*Does so.*) He smokes. He doesn't know what to say. (*He plays with his cap, taking it off, putting it on again.*) He plays with his hat. He hasn't changed.

SOL: Good to see you, sister. You're a sight for sore eyes. She smiles. (*Does so.*)

MIMI: Thank you.

SOL: She's relaxing. (*Pause.*)

MIMI: Pause....Did you write anything while you were there?

SOL: Not a word. I read junk novels. She wants to laugh.

MIMI: Ah. Any...new recruits?

SOL: All I ever did with the other inmates was watch TV.

MIMI: He knows what I am thinking.

SOL: She is disappointed.

MIMI: I thought maybe....

SOL: She recovers. (*She smiles.*) She's smiling.

MIMI: It was four months this time, right? (*Crosses to fire, pokes at it.*)

SOL: Four dreary, long, hellish months. She pokes at the fire.

MIMI: I'm sorry. (*She comes back.*)

SOL: She touches his face. (*She does so.*) He sighs. (*He does so.*) Ah, well...free board and room.

MIMI: (*She laughs.*) The cynic speaks. (*He laughs.*) He laughs.

SOL: Nothing like a prison stint to make you a died-in-the-wool cynic!

MIMI: I suppose. Do you regret doing it? (*She sits.*)

SOL: It had to be done. It's the only thing that will make those bastards believe we're serious about stopping the arms race.

MIMI: He still speaks with conviction.

SOL: We have to be willing to put our lives on the line. She doesn't believe him.

MIMI: You still believe that?

SOL: Of course.

MIMI: And you'd do it again?

SOL: Hell, yes. (*Leans back in his chair.*)

MIMI: He leans back in his chair. Ah, Sol, I admire your. . . .

SOL: She searches for the right word.

MIMI: . . .grit. (*Drinks to him.*)

SOL: She drinks to him. (*He laughs.*)

MIMI: He laughs.

SOL: We will win you know. (*He drinks.*)

MIMI: He drinks. I hope you're right.

SOL: It's the business to be done, the task at hand. (*Pause.*)

MIMI: Pause. . . . You know, to tell you the truth, I felt a little envious of you. When I was arrested I got off with three days of community service. Served it. . . .

SOL: (*Interrupting*). . . working at the food shelves.

MIMI: Yes. He's heard all this before. (*She crosses her legs.*)

SOL: She crosses her legs.

MIMI: I was actually rather disappointed. I thought a short time in prison would somehow. . . purify me, burn away some of the fat around my brain. (*She looks away.*) Does that make any sense to you?

SOL: Sure it does. She looks at him. (*She looks at him. She looks away.*) She looks away. I used to think the same thing, even enjoyed my one and two day stints, but four months of it is like being drugged, being driven into unconsciousness! She looks skeptical.

MIMI: I guess one only hears the more heroic tales. I remember Douglas saying that he meditated in his cell every day. Going to prison, he said, led him to God. Sounded promising. (*She drinks. He laughs.*) He laughs.

SOL: Douglas?! He wants us to think he's a goddamned saint! I don't believe him for a minute. He was probably masturbating.

MIMI: He wants me to laugh. (*She laughs.*)

SOL: She laughs. That's what keeps you going. That and sleeping. No, there's nothing holy about prison. I often felt like a bloody fool for being there.

Thought about giving up civil disobedience forever when I got out.

MIMI: And what would you do instead?

SOL: She makes a joke. (*He laughs.*)

MIMI: He laughs.

SOL: That's just it, isn't it? Organizing is the only thing I know how to do! (*They both laugh.*)

MIMI: He laughs.

SOL: (*Simultaneously*) She laughs.

SOL: So . . . it's back to the meeting hall.

Pause.

BOTH: Pause.

SOL: And what have you been up to?

MIMI: Not a lot. A few commercials. Small role at New Horizons. Lousy play — by an unknown. I expect he'll remain so.

SOL: She looks nervous.

MIMI: Pause.

SOL: She changes the subject.

MIMI: When's the next action?

SOL: April 17th.

MIMI: My birthday.

SOL: Ah, how old?

MIMI: Fifty. Half a century. A lot more than half a life, I suppose. Frightening.

SOL: You certainly don't look fifty.

MIMI: (*She rises.*) He lies. Aren't you sweet.

SOL: She rises. (*She kisses him on the top of his head.*)

MIMI: She kisses him lightly and exits for the kitchen. (*Does so.*) I have to check the roast; be right back. He doesn't know what it means to be fifty. Fill up your drink?

SOL: Thanks. (*She comes back for his glass. Exits. He lights up a new cigarette,* paces.) He lights up a new cigarette, paces. (*Calling out to her*) We're aiming for a thousand at the turn-out, three or four hundred arrests. The Berrigans will come to speak. Walter Harrison is writing a feature on it in the Sunday magazine section sometime in March. Will you be there?

MIMI: (*Returning*) He's avoiding me.

SOL: She returns with fresh drinks.

MIMI: On my birthday?

SOL: Hell, yes! what better way to spend it? (*He slaps her on her back.*)

MIMI: He slaps her on the back.

SOL: We'll sing Happy Birthday to you in the paddy wagon on the way down to jail. (*He laughs.*)

MIMI: He laughs.

SOL: She doesn't laugh.

MIMI: I'll consider it.

BOTH: They drink. (*They drink.*)

Pause.

BOTH: Pause.

MIMI: Don't you ever. . .crack?

SOL: Yes. Twice. (*She laughs.*) Now she laughs.

MIMI: Only twice? (*He laughs.*) He laughs.

SOL: Once when I was breaking up with my wife and we. . . .

MIMI: I remember.

SOL: She interrupts.

MIMI: We had a celebration at the river, got drunk out of our minds. (*She laughs.*)

SOL: We had a fight — the final fight. (*She looks away.*) She's looking away. It was Tuesday night, and I had made dinner which I rarely did. Spaghetti. It was over cooked. . .limp. And the sauce wasn't cooked enough. Undone carrots, raw hamburger — awful! (*He laughs.*)

MIMI: He laughs.

SOL: She doesn't laugh.

MIMI: He's trying to protect me by laughing. (*He laughs again.*)

SOL: She came home from teaching — a job that supported us both. (*Pause. They drink.*)

MIMI: Pause.

SOL: She's careful not to share an opinion about that. I was trying to get the stuff on the table and I was bitching and moaning about the newsletter which was late coming out and the fight I'd had that afternoon with Tim Shanks at the Turn Toward Peace office about whether to let people with beards join the walk on Saturday — can you believe it? (*He laughs.*)

MIMI: He laughs. (*She laughs.*)

SOL: Now she's laughing. (*Drinks.*) And then Sherri started in on me. She gets up. (*She doesn't.*)

MIMI: He gets up. (*Pause. He gets up.*)

SOL: "Why don't you get out if you hate it so?" "Why don't you do something constructive with your life?" "When are you going to finish your book?" Etcetera, etcetera. (*He drinks.*)

MIMI: He drinks. (*He drinks again.*) He drinks. He drinks again. (*He drinks, turns toward her.*) He looks right at her.

SOL: I cracked. I picked up the pot of spaghetti which was still sitting in the boiling water on the stove and I threw it at her. I did. I did that.

Pause.

MIMI: Pause.

SOL: She's not fazed. It scalded her head and. . .burned. . .the side of her face. She put her head under the cold water faucet in the sink and I said I was sorry. I'm sorry. I'm sorry.

MIMI: He thinks he has to apologize to me.

SOL: But it was too late. So here I was working for peace, and inside I was. . .pulling the trigger. . .without thinking twice. My world crashed.

MIMI: She thinks: what about her world?

SOL: She's not buying it. (*She looks away.*) She looks away. (*Pause, puts cigarette out.*) We split, and I didn't give a damn about anything. The human race could go to hell for all I cared. I certainly wasn't into saving its ass anymore.

MIMI: She breathes. You left the movement?

SOL: For awhile. . . .

MIMI: He looks grim.

SOL: Applied for a few teaching jobs. (*He laughs.*)

MIMI: He laughs.

SOL: Thought I could hide myself in an ivory tower in some little town 'til I was old enough to retire.

MIMI: I can't quite picture you there. (*She makes some characteristic nervous gesture with her hands.*)

SOL: She makes that old familiar gesture with her hands. (*He laughs.*)

MIMI: He laughs. (*She laughs.*)

SOL: Neither could the administrators of the colleges I applied to! (*He lights up another cigarette. Pause.*)

MIMI: So?

SOL: So. . .she's starting to relax. So an old girlfriend came through town on her way to Mississippi and the civil rights movement. I took her to bed one night and the next day I hopped on the bus with her. She thinks. . .?

MIMI: He wonders what she thinks of that.(*She shakes her head.*)

SOL: She shakes her head. (*Smokes.*)

MIMI: He smokes. (*He sits.*)

SOL: In the South I found out what real courage was. . .in the face of hideous brutality, and our own. . .inadequacy. Suddenly my problems seemed. . .ridiculously insignificant. She's heard this all before.

MIMI: Yes. I know what you mean.

SOL: It was a great fight.

MIMI: Honorable.

SOL: I never felt so. . .unambiguous. . .is that the word?. . .

MIMI: He wants her to find the right word for him.

SOL: . . . about what I was doing.

MIMI: And, after all, you won.

SOL: After a fashion. Is she laughing at him?

MIMI: We all came down to meet you at the bus — the conquering hero returns home, then we drove you out to the river, singing the whole way. . . and threw you in. Do you remember?

SOL: Yes. She hasn't forgotten. (*He smokes.*)

MIMI: He smokes. To the struggle! (*She drinks.*)

SOL: To the struggle! (*He drinks.*) That's why we have to get thousands climbing over the fences, getting arrested — make those bastards listen to us again.

MIMI: Sometimes I think we might be going about it the wrong way. (*She frowns.*)

SOL: She frowns. (*He looks away.*)

MIMI: He looks away.

SOL: Oh? How so?

MIMI: I don't know. Perhaps the business at hand is different than we imagine. (*She shakes her head.*)

SOL: She's shaking her head in that weird way of hers. It's what it's always been — a war against oppression.

MIMI: Sometimes I think it's more . . . personal.

SOL: That's what they'd like us to believe.

MIMI: He talks about "them" as if he knew them. . . . Another drink? (*Goes to kitchen.*)

SOL: She's changing the subject.

MIMI: (*Calling back*) What was the second time?

SOL: The second time?

MIMI: You cracked. You said, "Twice."

SOL: Oh, yes. That. (*Mimi returns with the bottle and ice, pours drinks for both of them.*) She returns with the whiskey. Thanks.

MIMI: Don't mention it. The second time?

SOL: Three years ago. You remember. At the height of the spring action. That little twit. . .what was her name?

MIMI: He expects me to remember her name.

SOL: With the short blonde hair and the scarf she always wore around her head like some bloody bandage? Maybe she needed it to hold her brains together. (*Laughs*.)

MIMI: He laughs. (*She laughs*.) Oh, yes. . .Karen. Karen what's-her-name. . .Wild-whatever. . .Oh, God, one of those names.

SOL: Wildflower! (*He laughs*.)

MIMI: Yes.

SOL: She laughs. (*Mimi laughs a half-swallowed laugh*.) That was a laugh? (*Drinks*.) How could I have forgotten? The name alone should have given me a clue.

MIMI: Love and light?

SOL: Yes. God give me darkness!

MIMI: (*Laughs*.) Remind me. I was on tour for a few weeks in the middle of all that. (*Sits*.)

SOL: She wanted me to re-structure the power imbalance of the group, encourage new members, invite more women into the center. . . .

MIMI: Sounds innocent enough. . . .

SOL: . . .have meetings about our lost spirituality. (*Drinks*.) She looks offended.

MIMI: I see.

SOL: God save me from missionaries!

MIMI: I'll try to remember. (*Drinks*.)

SOL: She takes his words personally. She drinks. And I became the target.

MIMI: That's right. It's coming back.

SOL: And the issues were forgotten.

MIMI: Oh, yes. . .the game of shoot the leader.

SOL: Right. She takes this very lightly. I was "too power-hungry." I was "too woman-hating." I was "manipulative" and "dangerous." In short, a pig.

MIMI: He takes this very seriously.

SOL: Two weeks before the action it all came out. She had gotten a little group together. They all stood behind her, and she lashed out at me with the fury of Medusa.

MIMI: Wildflower Medusa? (*Laughs.*)

SOL: She makes a joke.

MIMI: She hated her father.

SOL: No doubt.

MIMI: You were a stand-in.

SOL: I never applied for the job.

MIMI: She was not totally sane, as I recall.

SOL: She's humoring me. Unfortunately many people failed to notice that small flaw in her.

MIMI: He's angry. I'm sorry that happened to you.

SOL: It knocked the ground out from under me.

MIMI: (*Laughs.*) I've had similar experiences — divorces, losses.

SOL: She's laughing. I wanted to die. (*He drinks.*)

MIMI: He drinks. (*She lifts her glass.*)

SOL: She lifts her glass.

MIMI: I'm so glad you didn't! (*Laughs.*)

SOL: She doesn't drink.

MIMI: He's really angry.

SOL: No one came to my rescue. (*He drinks.*)

MIMI: He drinks. And drinks. Well, it's over now.

SOL: No one stood in my shoes.

MIMI: He's been angry for a long, long time. Are you hungry?

SOL: What?

MIMI: Hungry. I have a roast in the oven. And boiled new potatoes with parsley and butter. I know you're a meat and potatoes man. (*She laughs, rises.*)

SOL: She is a stranger to him.

MIMI: Why isn't he laughing?

Pause. She sits.

MIMI: Pause. It will be awhile yet. Would you like something to knash on? Some stilton? Crackers? She is trying to rescue him.

SOL: What? She's talking to him as if he were someone else. (*He looks at her.*)

MIMI: He looks up.

SOL: Oh, no thanks. She is patronizing me. I'm fine with this. (*Holds his glass up.*)

MIMI: She didn't mean to hurt him.

SOL: Good friends, good drink, good conversation. What else could a man want?

BOTH: (*Laugh.*) They laugh.

Pause.

BOTH: Pause.

MIMI: He lights a cigarette. (*He does.*)

SOL: Do you ever think about getting married again?

MIMI: Married? Oh, God, no. Twice is enough for me. Unless. . . .

SOL: She's not going to say it. Unless?

MIMI: I was going to say unless Mister Right comes along. . . .

SOL: She did say it.

MIMI: . . .but it seems rather far-fetched. (*She laughs.*)

SOL: She laughs. Her laugh is unreal.

MIMI: You?

SOL: Me? No. No. It never seems to quite work out that way for me. . .with the ladies.

MIMI: She believes him. Ah.

Pause.

BOTH: Pause.

MIMI: He changes the subject.

SOL: How are your children?

MIMI: Good. Good. Wilfred is in graduate school, you know.

SOL: Law school, right?

MIMI: Yes.

SOL: We need more good lawyers.

MIMI: Yes.

SOL: And Tammy?

MIMI: Still at Smith.

SOL: That's good. Doing well?

MIMI: Lost. She's lost.

SOL: Problems with classes?

MIMI: Oh, no. She's doing well. A's and B's. Her professors love her. She has friends. A boyfriend of sorts. (*Pause.*) Pause. . . . I worry about her though. You know how mothers are. He doesn't. (*She rubs her neck.*)

SOL: She's rubbing her neck. He thinks maybe he should rub it for her. It's the times. (*He smokes.*)

MIMI: Yes — the times. He's smoking.

SOL: She might cry.

MIMI: Don't let him touch her.

SOL: He touches her. (*He does.*)

MIMI: She moves away. (*She does. She laughs.*)

SOL: She laughs.

MIMI: What difference does it make anyway? We march, we leaflet, we sit down in front of the gates, we get arrested, we. . . .

(*The next ten lines are spoken quickly, almost overlapping.*)

SOL: She's very upset.

MIMI: He wishes he could do something.

SOL: She's losing control. (*He reaches out to touch her.*)

MIMI: He reaches out to touch her again. (*He aborts the move.*)

SOL: She doesn't move.

MIMI: He looks away.

SOL: She looks away.

MIMI: It's useless.

SOL: Mimi. . . .

MIMI: I'm useless.

SOL: Mimi, how can you say that about yourself? You have helped so many —your family, the movement, your audiences. You know lots of people think. . . .

MIMI: (*Interrupting*) I make commericals, Sol!

SOL: She's yelling at me.

MIMI: Do you think I keep my children in college and live in this apartment and buy these clothes by strutting across the stage? "Oh, Herb, you have ring around the collar, again." "My family's health is the most important thing to me, that's why we drink Tang." God! It's all so. . . .

SOL: She feels helpless.

MIMI: . . . empty.

SOL: Why do you put yourself down like that, Mimi? She won't look at him. You're a good actor. I'll never forget THE SEAGULL, or your HEDDA. Or your performance as Willie Loman's wife. . . .

MIMI: Oh, that. . . "Attention must be paid." He talks about her work. (*Rises, moves away.*)

SOL: Yes. . . yes. . . "Attention must be paid."

MIMI: What about her?

SOL: To you, too, Mimi.

MIMI: Oh, God, what's come over me?

SOL: She's looking right at him now.

MIMI: It must be the whiskey.

SOL: He's supposed to cheer her up. (*Laughs, rises.*)

MIMI: He laughs.

SOL: (*Sings.*) "Rye whiskey, rye whiskey, and wild, wild women...."

BOTH: (*Laugh.*) They laugh.

SOL: Love 'em and leave 'em! (*Laughs.*)

MIMI: He laughs. Yes.

SOL: He empties his glass. (*He does.*)

MIMI: She gets the bottle and fills his glass. Ice? (*Goes to him, fills his glass.*)

SOL: (*Nods.*) She drops the ice in...one, two, three. Thanks!

MIMI: Forgive me?

SOL: For what?

MIMI: This...outburst.

SOL: What are friends for? (*They drink.*)

Pause.

BOTH: Pause.

SOL: She's waiting for me to say something. (*He laughs.*)

MIMI: Sol sits. (*They both sit.*)

SOL: Mimi sits. (*Laughs.*)

MIMI: He laughs.

SOL: We go back a long time, Mimi. (*He smokes.*)

MIMI: He smokes.

SOL: I remember carrying Wilfred on my back when he was a baby, as we marched into Washington D.C. over twenty years ago.

MIMI: Yes. To hear Martin Luther King's dream, which we hitched on to our own so we could swagger through the glorious sixties with all our feathers blazing. (*Sol laughs.*) He is laughing. (*She drinks to him.*)

SOL: And swagger we did! And now...here we are. And you're almost fifty. Here's to fifty more, fighting the good fight. (*He drinks.*)

MIMI: He drinks.

SOL: She doesn't look at him.

MIMI: Yes. If only I knew for sure what the good fight is. (*She gets up, crosses to window, looks out.*)

SOL: She goes to the window. She watches the snow.

MIMI: I've spent my whole life trying to save people, you know. It's a strange way to fill a life when you think about it. Almost never works.

SOL: What?

MIMI: The business of trying to save people.

SOL: He waits for her to go on.

MIMI: Pause.

Pause.

SOL: He watches her.

MIMI: I mean you almost always fail, don't you.

Pause. Sol gets up, moves away.

MIMI: Pause. I remember, when I was around nine — that's when it started. I think I was nine, eight maybe, eight or nine. I found a tiny bird lying under the Maple tree in the back yard. A baby. He was a robin, I think. Perhaps a sparrow. He must have fallen out of his nest. He was so young, his feathers were still wet. He looked. . .naked. I didn't want to touch him. He looks at her.

SOL: (*He looks away.*) He looks away.

MIMI: He should. . . .

SOL: He thinks he should. . . .

MIMI: Pause. But I picked him up anyway. His little heart was pumping so fast, I could see his chest beating in and out, in and out. And his large eyes, staring at me, popping out of his head like a frog's. Or like someone who drinks too much.

SOL: She makes a joke.

MIMI: He laughs. (*He does.*) I held him in the palm of my hand and took him into my house and put him in a box with some scraps of flannel for a bed. I fed him sugar water with an eye dropper and I talked to him. His feathers filled out and he began to talk back: Chir-up, chir-up...not exactly a song, you know, but sounds at any rate. I knew I should give him his freedom, but I was reluctant to let him go. (*She turns away.*)

SOL: She looks away.

MIMI: I had grown fond of him...attached. Not so much to the frailty of the bird, as to my own sense of purpose, I suppose. As he became stronger, I fed him bird seed softened in warm milk, and I put a small bowl of fresh water in his box for him to bathe in. One morning when I came downstairs, he was silent. At first I thought he had found a way out. But then I noticed his limp body at the side of the bowl, his neck, strangely elongated, hanging over the edge, so that his head reached down and was entirely covered by the water. He had drowned. (*She looks at him.*)

SOL: She looks at him.

MIMI: He says nothing.

SOL: (*To himself*) It happens. (*He sits.*)

MIMI: So what had been the use, I wondered. Pause.

SOL: Pause.

MIMI: Then when I was twelve, thirteen perhaps, I went to a new school.

SOL: She tells another story.

MIMI: It was actually a very old school, a convent converted into a junior high. But new for me. She wishes he would stop her. There was a girl named Eileen. She was very large for her age, although she was fifteen ... retarded perhaps...and almost unbearably plain. She was unkempt. She had long, stringy brown hair, and she dressed in old clothes that were much too small for her — layers of clothes, skirts over skirts, blouses over blouses, prints and faded flowers.

SOL: He thinks perhaps he should stop her.

MIMI: Her family was poor. They were tenant farmers on a small plot at the edge of town. There were many in her family...kids and chickens. They all ran loose in the barnyard. One had the impression of layers of dirt on her skin, like the layers of clothing. The other children said that she was crazy. There were stories whispered in the playground...about knives, incest...No one would speak to her.

SOL: She looks away.

MIMI: I befriended her.

SOL: She's. . . .

MIMI: I took pity on her. I gave her books to read. I drew pictures for her. I made up stories about how I would discover that she was a great artist, and would take her away from her squalid hovel and despicable life and make her famous.

SOL: She. . . .

MIMI: Then one afternoon, when I knew my mother would be gone, I invited her home. We went up to my bedroom and I showed her my scrapbooks and my blue silk china doll who always sat primly in the center of my bed. And I read from my diary to her. I don't remember how it came about exactly, but in the course of the afternoon's events, we ended up lying on the bed together, with no clothes on. Some pretense, I suppose, a game, like "hospital" or "movies." And then she began to touch my newly formed breasts and move her fingers in places I hardly knew existed, with such skill I knew she had had experiences I had only fantasized about. And I could not muster up the words to tell her to stop. Pause. When she left, I lay there on the bed.

SOL: She's looking at me.

MIMI: He's looking at me. (*Pause. She sits.*)

SOL: She sits.

MIMI: I remember suddenly seeing the doll lying, where she had been thrown. . .carelessly. . .on the floor, her blue silk dress flung up over her head, her alabaster legs spewed apart. . .lifelessly. And then I bathed myself. For several hours. I sat in the bathtub and scrubbed my skin, trying to wash away the dirt. . .my sense of loss. Pause. Soon after that she disappeared. I didn't care. I had lost interest in. . .saving her. (*She gets up.*)

SOL: She gets up.

MIMI: He gets up. (*He does.*)

SOL: He laughs. (*He does.*)

MIMI: He takes his drink with him.

SOL: When I was about that same age, I had a job as a delivery boy for our local butcher, Zalmin Abramson. He used to take me in his back room. . . God, I haven't thought about him in years!. . . and jack me off. (*Mimi turns away.*) She's looking away. Maybe he did it to all the local boys.MIMI: She thinks: maybe Sol was fat.

SOL: (*Laughs.*) He laughs.

MIMI: Maybe he was ugly.

SOL: He smokes.

MIMI: Did you despise him?

SOL: Hell, no. He was just getting his rocks off. He was a man, a good man. He didn't harm anyone.

MIMI: Yes. Of course. (*Angrily*) Pause! It doesn't seem quite the same. But then. . . I suppose it wasn't Eileen that I despised either.

Pause.

BOTH: Pause.

MIMI: Sometimes I think about her when we sit at these interminable meetings trying to decide how to reach out to the people whose countrysides we are devastating, whose women and children we are murdering. (*She looks at him.*)

SOL: She looks at him.

MIMI: We're helpless, aren't we? The devastations go on. . . the murders go on. . . But we argue among ourselves and we sing our freedom songs and go to jail and send brigades of bandages and books to our comrades, who want only to survive, to live their lives more. . . spaciously.

SOL: She's yelling at me again.

MIMI: And I wonder whether we're not more attached to our own goodness than to their struggle.

SOL: He is a stranger to her.

MIMI: And were we to look into the eyes of these "comrades" would we see them clearly?

SOL: He drinks.

MIMI: Would we love them if we were to see them, not as victims, but as survivors. . . .

SOL: He smokes.

MIMI: Survivors who make our own attempts at making order of our lives look ludicrous?

SOL: He smokes.

MIMI: What if we were to see the pity in their eyes — for us?

SOL: He drinks.

MIMI: Pity at best. . . .

SOL: He smokes.

MIMI: . . . more likely contempt.

SOL: He smokes. He. . . .

MIMI: Pause.

SOL   Pause. (*Pause.*)

MIMI: Once I went to a cabin on the Northern lakes. I went alone. Stayed for almost a month up there, seeing no one. I was miserable. My second marriage had just ended in shambles. My career was washed up. I had no offers for roles; commericals seemed the only avenue left open to me. And how I hated them! Oh, not for ethical reasons, as you might think, but because of the long, boring hot hours in front of the camera, the inane conversations. I felt desolate. So I went to a friend's cabin, read cheap novels, drank cheap wine and cried myself into a paroxysm of self-pity.

SOL: He laughs. (*Does so.*)

MIMI: He laughs.

SOL: He drinks.

MIMI: One night. . . I have never told anyone this. . . I went out to the edge of the lake. It was a black, moonless night. You couldn't tell where the lake left off and the sky began. I sat there peering into the darkness, the black hole of the night. I thought: so this is where it ends. Terror, such as I had never experienced before, crept into my bones, and ran up and down the surface of my skin like cut glass. Inside and out — no release. I shut my eyes — black silence. I opened my eyes — the same. Empty. At the root. I thought: this is what we all fear. This is why we go to war, and why we march, and why we heal our wounds — to fend off this ghoulish emptiness. And so I sat, for maybe an hour or so, wrapped in fear. It was then that I began to notice that I was. . . awake. Fear had jarred me awake. Every pore and sinew of my body was alert. I thought: perhaps before this moment I have always been asleep. As that thought passed through my mind, I began to be aware of a beam of light, descending through the air...a thick light...a suffocating light, isolated and remote. I found it difficult to breathe. I thought: I am going to die now. It was as if only death, only a complete surrender of all my living tissue would be enough to meet this...lucent...alien. It continued to come relentlessly through the blackness toward the place where I sat. And then — without a moment's hesitation — it entered me...like a lover. Imperceptibly the fear drained out of me...leaving...without a trace. Slowly I began to see...as if the light were now behind my eyes, illuminating everything. In the shadows, in the edges of the leaves, in the blades of grass, in the markings on the glass top of the lake, I began to see thousands of tiny movements, like the life deep down inside of things...shimmering. Then suddenly everything was lit...from inside. And what I saw was nature being well, being whole. I saw everything in order, things appearing exactly as they should. And I was totally in love — as I have never been in love with any man — with life itself.

Pause.

MIMI: Pause.

SOL: Pause.

MIMI: Pause.

SOL: Pause.

MIMI: Pause.

Pause.

MIMI: I thought after that everything would be changed. And so it was for a short while, a few weeks perhaps. I saw the radiance inside of things — my plants, my children, the old women at the bus stop. But numbness has a way of creeping back into the heart, and soon it was gone. It became a memory, another thing to hang on to, no longer real. I began — way down — to despise myself again. And the longing which had led me to that spot pressed against my bones...like a shroud.

SOL: He smokes.

MIMI: Oh, Sol, it isn't the earth we want to save, or the victims of our foreign policies, or even the Eileens or the wounded birds...it is ourselves.

SOL: He smokes.

MIMI: We long to tear off this skin, this shell that we have locked ourselves into as snugly as we lock up tigers at the zoo. We long to tear off pretense to find out who we are. Who's in there? (*She pounds at her chest.*)

SOL: He smokes.

MIMI: Who is it really who is so afraid to trust? Look at us!

SOL: He smokes.

MIMI: We think we are free — free to give our minds and our hearts to the service of freeing others. (*She grabs him by the sweater, shakes him.*) But we are prisoners! You got out of jail today, but you are as locked into your little view of good and evil, right and wrong, as if the jailer had thrown away the key and left you locked in your cell forever! (*She pounds on him hysterically.*) Don't you understand?! Do you know what I am talking about?

SOL: She. . . .

MIMI: He. . . .

SOL: Pause, pause, pause, Mimi, Mimi, Sssshhhhh, sssshhhh, there, there, calm down. (*He holds her.*)

MIMI: (*Softly*) Pause.

SOL: She sits, she sits, sits. (*She does.*) Pause. These things you talk about . . . greater men and women than either of us have driven themselves crazy over such things.

MIMI: Oh, God, I'm sorry. I'm sorry. I shouldn't have said those things. I didn't know what I was saying. Forgive me.

SOL: Don't be ridiculous. What are friends for, eh? Pause.

MIMI: Pause.

SOL: You o.k.?

MIMI: Yes. Yes.

SOL: He drinks.

MIMI: (*Gets up.*) I'll go check the dinner.

SOL: No. . .please. . .I should really be going. (*Puts his cigarette out.*)

MIMI: Oh?

SOL: Yes. . .Peter's at the office and I said I'd stop by. . . .

MIMI: But the roast beef...potatoes. ...

SOL: They fed me before I left. I'm not really hungry. Do you mind?

MIMI: No. No...Do whatever you...think, you. ...

SOL: Will you be o.k.?

MIMI: Me? Oh, of course. I'm fine. Will you be o.k.?

SOL: Me? (*Laughs.*) I'm terrific. (*He slaps her on the back.*)

MIMI: He slaps her on the back.

SOL: Good friends, good drink, good conversation. What more could a man want? (*Laughs.*)

MIMI: Right. (*Laughs.*)

SOL: She laughs.

MIMI: Of course. (*Sits.*)

SOL: She sits.

MIMI: Shall I see you to the door?

SOL: No...No, don't bother. (*Goes to the door, puts on coat and boots.*)

MIMI: He's going.

SOL: See you Wednesday at the project meeting?

MIMI: Wednesday is it? Of course. I'll be there.

SOL: Thanks for the drinks.

MIMI: Right. Anytime. And welcome home.

SOL: Keep your chin up sister!

MIMI: Yes. You too.

SOL: He leaves. (*He does.*)

MIMI: (*Calling after him*) Chin up! Pause...I did it again. Oh, God, she did it again.

WILLIAM S. YELLOW ROBE, JR.

Sneaky

WILLIAM S. YELLOW ROBE, JR. is an enrolled member of the Assisniboine Tribe of the Fort Peck Indian Reservation in northeast Montana. He was born and reared in traditional Indian ways in Wolf Point, Montana, where he later graduated from high school. He is the second youngest of nine children raised by his mother, Mina Rose. His father served on the Tribal Council and co-founded A & S Industries, the largest single private employer in Montana. Yellow Robe later attended Northern Montana College in Havre and the University of Montana in Missoula, where he studied history, journalism, and the performing arts.

William S. Yellow Robe, Jr.'s interest in the theater goes all the way back to his childhood. He wrote his first play in the sixth grade. Although many of his plays and stories deal with traditional Indian themes and concepts, he has also written for children's theaters and most recently a play about AIDS. In the past three years he has written five commissioned plays. Productions of his work have been mounted (under his direction) at Ensemble Studio Theatre in New York and at the American Conservatory Theatre in San Francisco. His play, *Taking Aunty to the Wake*, was produced at the Purple Mountain Theatre in St. Ignatius, Montana in the summer of 1989. *The Independence of Eddie Rose* will be produced by the Group Theatre in Seattle in the summer of 1990 and co-sponsored by the Good Will Games.

Yellow Robe was chosen as a 1988 Jerome Fellow and served a nine-month residency at the Playwrights' Center in Minneapolis. Currently, as the only playwriting winner of a 1989 Princess Grace Award, he is serving as Literary Manager at the Group Theatre.

His works include: *Independence of Eddie Rose, Wink-Dah, Sneaky, Harvest, My Walks with Grandma, The People, The Breaking of Another Circle, The Pendleton Blanket, A Great Thing, Taking Aunty to the Wake, Wa-Kik-Na,* and *A Coyote's Tale.* His works include plays for childrens theatre and he is a published short story writer. He is very interested in writing scripts for film.

His wife, Diane Ruth Lamar Yellow Robe, acts as his Business Manager.

———————

SNEAKY IS A play about relationships among and between Native American Indians and Non-Indians on a Northeastern Montana reservation. Death and how it is viewed by some in each of the two cultures becomes the focal point for the action experimentally illustrating the major conflict in view points.

———————

I WOULD LIKE TO thank the following people for allowing me to share *Sneaky* with the people: Ms. Roberta Uno-Thelwell, New World Theatre, University of Massachusetts, Amherst, Massachusettes. Mr. Tim Bond, Multi Cultural Playwrights' Festival, Seattle Group Theatre, Seattle, Washington. Mr. Donovan Marley, Denver Center for Performing Arts, Denver, Colorado. Ms. Diane Ruth Lamar Yellow Robe. Mr. Stanley and Mrs. Mina Yellowrobe, Wolf Point, Montana.

These people have made it possible for me to share this play with people from across the country. Thank you once again.

— *William S. Yellow Robe, Jr.*

In Prologue:

FRANK ROSE: A young Native American Indian child, who is ten, or twelve years old.

GRANDMOTHER: A Native American Indian woman who is in her late sixties.

In Play:

FRANK ROSE: A Native American Indian who is in his mid-thirties.

ELDON ROSE: A Native American Indian who is in his early thirties. He is the middle brother of the family.

KERMIT ROSE: A Native American Indian who is in late twenties.

JACK KENCE: A white male, in his early forties. He is second generation at the funeral home.

Prologue

TIME: Late morning. Early 1950's
PLACE: Outside a small stucco house

The yard has boundaries made of cut and uncut weeds. A small fire pit is located several feet from the house. The sky is cloudy and creates a gray colored day. The wind has a soft wail to it. Located next to the fire pit is a large cardboard box. A piece of plywood serves as a lid for the box. The grandson, Frank Rose sits near the box. Thunder rolls in the sky and the boy farts.)

GRANDMOTHER: Oh-Quaw. (*She enters and carries a metal folding chair, a small piece of rope and a knife.*)

FRANK: Grandma?

GRANDMOTHER: Yes.

FRANK: Grandma, why, why do we have to do this? Why couldn't we have chicken, turkey, or Dinty Moore stew?

GRANDMOTHER: This is the way it should be done. We have always done it this way. When I was a little girl. I was taught by my mother. This is the way puppy is to be prepared. (*She sets the chair down and unfolds it. She places the blade of the knife into the ground and holds the rope.*) I suppose, Dinty Moore stew. (*She uses the chair to get to her knees.*)

FRANK: No, no, not that grandma. Why do we have to eat puppy?

GRANDMOTHER: It is the way of our people.

FRANK: I don't like it. . .I don't like puppy.

GRANDMOTHER: Oh! When have you ever tasted puppy before? Huh?

FRANK: When grandpa died.

GRANDMOTHER: I suppose. . .You were too young to remember. (*Pause. Chuckles.*) And you have never eaten tripe before.

FRANK: I love my puppy.

GRANDMOTHER: And I do too. You will enjoy it's warm juicy meat in your belly. Don't bother me now grandson. (*She picks up the rope and prays with it, holding the rope in the air. She finishes and sets the rope down. She picks up the box and raises it in the air. The box wavers in the air. She steadies the box and prays again. After she finishes, she sets the box down. We hear a whimpering of a puppy from the box.*) Grandson, we eat puppy in honor of our people. Those who have died, or are receiving a new name or other honors. Those who have died and must continue on another journey are fed from our giving. (*Pause.*) There was a time when the people used the dog to carry their belongings for them. . . And a time when we had a great winter and the people were starving. Because provisions promised by treaty from the government never arrived. And many of them died. A lot of them were your grandparents. (*Pause.*) In this winter, we could not bury the people in our old ways. . . our ways. And in the whiteman's burial we had to place them in the ground and cover them with dirt. We would be trapping their souls. This one winter, we didn't bury them in the ground like the whiteman wanted us to. The ground was too frozen and hard, thousands died one year. (*Pause.*) The next spring, one day, I was going to visit my cousins. I came by a little mound. I didn't know what it was, so I got closer to see. Then I saw this hole. It was a badger's hole. (*Pause.*) It was coming up and I wasn't sure at first, but he had something in his mouth. I looked real hard to see better. It was white whatever it was. As I got closer, I could see the mound was a huge grave. The badger held a hand in his mouth. When he seen me he charged me. Then he stopped and looked at me. In his eyes he was saying to me, 'See. You didn't take care of this person. You should have taken care of this one.' And then he turned and went back into his hole. (*Pause.*) We suffered a great loss. In time, the people had managed to feed themselves, their relations and even friends. They ate their dogs to live. Some of the people offered their dogs for a blessing of food. There was an answer from the Heavenly Father. . .Before the steamboats came. . .Long before the Black Robe Missions were serving their turkeys, cows and chickens.

FRANK: What about ray-shuns?

GRANDMOTHER: Oh my. What do you know about rations? Huh? Grandson?

FRANK: Rations are chop meat, macaronies, cheese, meatball stew, peanut butter and stuff like that.

GRANDMOTHER: There were no rations. That's not food any way. (*Pause.*) There are those people who eat dog regularly and some who don't eat it. (*Pause.*) Grandson, Frank. There are things you do not fully understand. We are not a mean, or cruel people. We do it in honor to those who have left us.

FRANK: I don't like it grandma.

GRANDMOTHER: It is something that has to be done. A dog is of more importance than a chicken. Have these chickens chased the ball for you? Or have they protected you from bad things? Greeted you when you came back from school? Have they kept you company when you were lonely, or sad? (*Pause.*) Your uncle. . . My son, has passed on. This puppy will accompany him on his journey.

FRANK: Uncle Jess? He and my puppy will go to heaven?

GRANDMOTHER: Yes. You can call it that.

FRANK: Oh. (*Pause.*) Grandma?

GRANDMOTHER: What?

FRANK: What about your cat Jiff?

GRANDMOTHER: What about her? (*The grandmother is slowly putting kindling into the firepit.*)

FRANK: Well. . .are we going to cook her up too?

GRANDMOTHER: Oh-quaw! No. Why do you ask?

FRANK: I don't know.

GRANDMOTHER: Are you trying to make fun of me?

FRANK: No. I was just asking. . .but why don't we cook Jiff up? She wouldn't mind.

GRANDMOTHER: That cat is useless. She is always getting into my sewing. Ripping or tearing something up. The only thing she is good for is keeping mice away from the house. But now, she is starting to like canned cat chow. She doesn't even care for table scraps. She is into something every day. . . .

FRANK: Well why don't you spank her, or get rid of her?

GRANDMOTHER: She is old. . .She keeps me company when you are in school. And there are time she makes me laugh. (*Pause.*)

FRANK: Grandma?

GRANDMOTHER: Yes, what is it?

FRANK: Will we offer another puppy the next time someone else dies?

GRANDMOTHER: Yes, but let's hope no one dies.

FRANK: I hope the next time we use Eldon's puppy.

GRANDMOTHER: Hee-ah! Don't think like that! You shouldn't talk like that!

FRANK: I'm sorry. . .but I miss my puppy. . .I'm going to miss him.

GRANDMOTHER: Yes. I know you will. Your puppy is the fattest and healthiest of the litter. You should feel good about your puppy being used. (*She starts the kindling on the fire.*)

FRANK: But no one asked me.

GRANDMOTHER: I know. No one asked your uncle if he wanted to die. (*Pause.*) When I was your age. I gave my puppy for a feast. I know it hurts to lose something you love. (*Pause.*) Is isn't for us, grandson, Frank. It's for your uncle. (*Pause.*) Grandson, you'll have another puppy. I'll get you one. (*The boy goes to her and hugs her.*)

FRANK: I love you grandma.

GRANDMOTHER: Wash-day, chi' nah.

FRANK: Washy-day, chi' nah.

FRANK: Oh, wash-day, chi' nah, grandma.

GRANDMOTHER: I must do this now. Our way. (*He backs away from her and she gets the puppy from the box and sets it on the ground. She holds it on its side with one hand and with the other hand she takes the rope and begins to wrap it around the dog's neck. Blackout. End of Prologue.*)

Scene One

TIME: Present day. Early morning. Fall.

Place: A small town on an Indian reservation.
The action takes place outside a small
stucco house, in the yard. Near a
housing project.

(*Frank Rose stands near a pile of clothing and other items. Not far from him is a second pile of clothes and small items. In the background is a house. It has a porch. The screendoor of the house is held open by a brick. There are some footsteps coming from within the house. The footsteps are Eldon Rose walking around inside of the house. Frank adjusts a large beaded belt buckle to ease the discomfort of his belly. He straightens the newly formed waist level.*)

ELDON: Hey! Hey! Frank. I've found her old buckskin dress. Boy does it look rugged, but not too shabby.

FRANK: Bring it out here and put in on the pile El'. (*Eldon comes from the house carrying an arm load of dresses and he is examining them. Frank takes a book of matches from his shirt pocket and lights one. He kneels down to light the larger pile of their mom's belongings.*) Our way.

ELDON: Hey Frank. Some of these dresses are still good. Is it all right if I take some of them to my wife? She could use the material.

FRANK: Hey! We're not supposed to keep this stuff, remember? It all has to be burned. Just toss them. . . .

ELDON: Frank! What the hell are you doing? Put that fire out! (*Races over to Frank.*)

FRANK: We're supposed to do this Eldon. Mom told me what she wanted to give to certain ones. The rest of mom's stuff is supposed to be burned. Just like we did for grandma, Dad, and now, mom.

ELDON: Frank. I was hoping we won't have to go through all of it.

FRANK: Why not? Grandma told me, you and Kermit, this should always be done. You haven't forgotten have you Eldon?

ELDON: No. Just wishing. I guess. (*Eldon returns to the clothes he has brought out from the house. From underneath the dresses, he removes two small boxes.*

One is a plastic tupper-ware case.) Frank. Look. (*Opens the tupper-ware case.*) It's her beadwork. Some of the beads are still pretty good. Could I keep them?

FRANK: Christ Eldon. Some of that stuff is pretty personal. She said what she didn't want has to be burned, the other stuff goes to 'give away.' That way there won't be a reason why mom will want to come back. (*Eldon returns to the house.*)

ELDON: All right Frank, all right. (*Frank begins to spread the fire to the pile. Eldon call from inside the house.*) You know what amazes me Frank? The house is still clean. What was it mom's dad used to say? 'You can be poor, but you don't have to live. . .holy shit. (*Comes to porch.*)

FRANK: Grandpa never said. . .What's wrong El'?

ELDON: This room. . .it's. . .filthy.

FRANK: Oh. You found Kermit's room. Mom used to clean it and then as she got older she just gave up on it.

ELDON: While we're at it. Let's burn the mattress he has in there.

FRANK: No. Just leave it where it's at.

ELDON: Why? He can find a new home.

FRANK: Don't forget, he deserves a few things.

ELDON: But he's not even here to help us! Christ. (*He walks to Frank.*) Does he even know what's happened?

FRANK: The cops told me at work. I asked them to tell him.

ELDON: And he still isn't here to help us? (*Pause.*) I hope everything doesn't go to 'give away.' I'd like to have. . .(*An object comes sailing by them.*)

FRANK: Watch it!

ELDON: Did you see that? What was it? Damn rock nearly hit me. Damn kids. . .

FRANK: Hello. (*Kermit enters carrying a broken baseball bat and he is singing.*)

KERMIT: Hey!

ELDON: Did you do that?

KERMIT: What?

ELDON: Throw this rock at me? (*Picks up the rock.*)

FRANK: El'. It's not a rock.

ELDON: Then what is it?

KERMIT: It's cowshit. Couldn't find a ball and don't want to hurt my bat with a rock.

ELDON: Oh Christ. You almost hit me! You almost hit me in the eye. . . .

KERMIT: Would've matched your other eye.

ELDON: Don't get smart with me Kermit. Christ! You're worse than my kids.

KERMIT: It was cowshit numbnut. You know, the stuff inside your head.

FRANK: Knock it off! Both of you!

KERMIT: Yeah. Are you okay Frank?

FRANK: Yeah.

ELDON: I'm fine too. What about you? Are you sober? I bet you're still on a toot. . . .

FRANK: Quiet Eldon. Go inside and bring out the rest of the stuff. There's plenty more.

ELDON: Me? Why doesn't he do it?

FRANK: Just do it, huh, Eldon.

ELDON: Christ. Okay. (*He starts to go to the house.*)

KERMIT: Good! Now we can talk real mean about you. Choc-ah-jah-luke!

ELDON: What? What did you say?

FRANK: Just go on in. He's just joking. (*Eldon continues to go to the house.*) I never knew you could speak Assiniboine. What the hell did you say?

KERMIT: It was 'Klingon' Frank. You know, 'beam me out of it Scotty.' (*Pause.*) Oh. Uh, Frank?

FRANK: What?

KERMIT: I went to your house this morning and your old lady told me you were here.

FRANK: Yeah.

KERMIT: Anyways, I was kinda' wondering. Can you loan me ten?

FRANK: What are you going to be doing? (*He takes a few bills from his wallet and gives them to Kermit.*)

KERMIT: I'm going into town.

FRANK: Okay.

KERMIT: I was playing in that softball tournament. Me, Ska Jones, Delmer Perry and a few others. We would've taken first but Ska and Delmer hit the lite beer too fast and by the time the game was almost over, they couldn't hit the ball. And there were all kinds of people there Frank. Some really nice looking babes too. I almost snagged one of them too.

FRANK: A ball?

KERMIT: Bend over. No Frank! A babe. I made the all star team too. Ska's still mad because they didn't pick him. And here, he was one of the guys who organized the tournament. And right after the game, this car, a cop, it came.... (*Pause.*) They told me.

FRANK: I knew they would. Mom's death took a lot out of me too.

KERMIT: I gotta' go. I told those guys I would meet them at the Long Horn. Are you going to be here for a while?

FRANK: Until we're finished.

KERMIT: Eldon too? (*Frank nods, 'yes.'*) That's good. (*He pockets the money and leaves.*)

FRANK: Hey! I want to talk to you. (*Kermit stops.*)

KERMIT: What? You want your money back. (*Crosses to Frank.*)

FRANK: No. Kind of take it, take it easy, huh? (*Eldon enters carrying two suitcases and a duffel bag.*)

KERMIT: What do you meant?

FRANK: There's going to be a lot of changes, and I want you in at least a halfassed decent condition when it's time to. ...

ELDON: Yeah Kermit. Not half shot like you are now.

KERMIT: Hey, man! I'm not drunk.

FRANK: He didn't say that.

KERMIT: I don't care what he says. I know what he means. (*Eldon takes a suitcase and throws it on the pile.*)

ELDON: There's no one here to help you with your habit. . . Sober you up anymore. (*Throws the suitcase on the pile.*)

KERMIT: Ahhhh! (*Sees the duffel bag.*) Hey! You throwing this away?

ELDON: Frank told me to. He wants it done this way.

KERMIT: But this is my old reliable. I took it everywhere with me, celebrations, basketball games, the works, man. . . .

ELDON: Then get a new one. You're young. It's shot. (*Kermit looks at Eldon and then at Frank and walks away.*)

KERMIT: Shit. (*He picks up a rocks and bats it.*)

ELDON: Frank?

FRANK: Don't be mad Kermit.

ELDON: Frank?

FRANK: You'll get another one.

ELDON: Frank?

FRANK: What?

ELDON: This one isn't bad. Can I have it?

FRANK: Are you going to save everything El'? I'd like to get this done.

KERMIT: He'll probably sell it to some damn white tourist.

ELDON: That is none of your business. At least, I have a business and Frank's a carpenter. What are you?

KERMIT: A skin.

ELDON: Yeah, right. It isn't yours anyway.

KERMIT: Shit head Eldon. (*Picks up another rock and swings.*)

ELDON: Frank. . . Frank. I'm just going to take what I deserve. Like a few things in mom's trunk.

FRANK: What?

ELDON: I'm going to take the things I deserve. Like a few things in mom's trunk.

KERMIT: What? No way! Those are the things she always kept. Remember Frank? Some of those things were given to her when she was a little girl. She always took care that stuff.

ELDON: Yeah. For us.

KERMIT: Don't let him take anything Frank.

FRANK: Do you want it?

KERMIT: No.

FRANK: Well then? (*Kermit walks away.*)

KERMIT: Damn.

FRANK: Go ahead. But if there's anything else El', you'd better check it with me.

ELDON: Can I have the rocking chair?

FRANK: Damn it El'. You should've brought a flatbed with you.

ELDON: Don't get mad. I was just asking.

KERMIT: Ahh, fuck, Frank. (*He picks up a rock and bats it.*)

ELDON: Why? What do you want?

FRANK: Nothing. But there are a few things she wants others to have.

ELDON: I'm going to take the things I have coming to me.

FRANK: She gave you some things?

ELDON: Yeah. And I want them. For my girls. I've earned them, like mom's dress. Remember? It was you, Frank, who got most of grandma's things. . . .

FRANK: They were given to me. I didn't claim them, hell, I didn't even ask for them.

ELDON: Did you ever sell some of that stuff? Like Grandpa's war bonnet?

FRANK: Hell no. Why should I?

ELDON: Are you going to sell it? I know a few people who would be interested in buying it.

FRANK: Hell no!

ELDON: Then why don't you put it in a museum? That's what we could do with her buckskin dress.

FRANK: Those people working in the museum wouldn't know how to take care of it. Why? Why do you want mom's buckskin dress?

ELDON: I deserve it! I have it coming to me. You got grandpa's war bonnet and Kermit got dad's little drum. I want mom's dress. I was the one who took care of her. I was the one who was there when she needed someone. . . .

FRANK: Is that what you're talking about? Being there? And being paid for it? Christ El, I don't know about you.

KERMIT: I was there for her too.

ELDON: It wasn't me who had her crying. Trying to be a tough guy. I didn't fight her like you did. And Frank, I wasn't the one who went drinking with dad.

KERMIT: Dad didn't want you around El', huh, Frank?

ELDON: But when you're drunk, no one wants you.

FRANK: Hold it hey! I helped mom. And when dad was low on cash I helped him.

ELDON: Did he need help spending it in the bars? Or being taxied by you from bar to bar?

FRANK: I won't. . . .

ELDON: You can't deny it. She was alone. Dad started drinking in his last few months and you joined him. She was left alone. She used to phone me and I would come over. And there would be this guy, raising hell with her. I would have to throw him out, stinking drunk. Dad would be there sometimes, but drunk, passed out in Kermit's room. And then sometimes you and dad would be fighting in the yard. (*Pause.*) Frank. Did you ever wonder why dad started drinking after seventeen years of not drinking?

FRANK: Sure I did El'. It bothered me. I did ask him one time and he wouldn't answer me. Told me not to worry about it. (*Pause.*) Do you know why?

ELDON: Yes. She didn't want me to know. Wouldn't tell me. Mom knew. She finally did. I can only remember a little bit of it. She said he was afraid.

FRANK: Afraid of what?

ELDON: It sounded strange to me then. The world they were raised in and how they were both raised. 'Two old Indians,' remember? It makes sense to me now. (*Pause.*) He was afraid he had forgotten how to die. Dad was afraid. Everything has changed so much and he wondered if he had changed. This world he lived in was different. How should he leave it? He thought maybe the other world had changed and he wondered, was afraid, if he could get there. That's the reason why he drank so much in his last few months. (*Pause.*) You didn't know, did you?

FRANK: No. It didn't come to me, but his time was near and he knew it. (*Pause.*) If you feel you deserve certain things, take them, but you remember. He deserves something. (*Points to Kermit.*) If you knew what you know today then, you should have told us. Packing around things like that.

ELDON: I didn't think you wanted to know from me. I thought. . . .

KERMIT: Fuck Eldon! You. . . .(*Pause.*) You should have told us that. You tell everyone everything else. I wanted to know why he pushed me away. All this time I thought it was me. That's the reason why I stayed away from home. I didn't want to get him mad. (*Pause.*) I remember coming home late one night and he was sitting at the kitchen table crying. I didn't know what to do. I asked him what was wrong. He didn't say anything. And here, you knew. (*Kermit exits.*) Damn.

ELDON: I didn't know. . . .I didn't know myself at the time. I. . . .(*Pause.*) Frank I didn't know.

FRANK: That's all right, but you remember, we're family. He has a right too.

ELDON: I do. . . .

FRANK: I'm going inside and start bringing out her bedding. We'll throw her matress on later. (*He goes into the house.*)

ELDON: I'll be right there. (*Blackout. End of Scene One.*)

Scene Two

TIME: It is in the evening.
PLACE: Outside of the small stucco house.
In the front yard.

(*The wind is softly blowing. Frank and Eldon are by a fire that is slowly burning out. There are a few small boxes around the brothers. Both brothers drink sodas. Their clothes are sweat stained.*)

FRANK: What do you think?

ELDON: I don't know. (*Pause.*) Yeah. I guess so.

FRANK: We did round everything up?

ELDON: Yeah...yeah. I did. (*Pause.*) What about the old blue steamer trunk?

FRANK: I found it in the root cellar.

ELDON: Too bad. Hey, what about those boxes of sewing patterns? Them too?

FRANK: Yeah. I got them too.

ELDON: The pictures?

FRANK: Not all.

ELDON: Good.

FRANK: I kept some of them. Take a look. (*Frank removes a small cigar box and hands it to Eldon. Eldon eagerly goes through it.*) She doesn't want anyone to have these. Burn them when you're done.

ELDON: The Smithsonian would want these...and this one, and that one...damn. You think we did right?

FRANK: Yeah, just like when the old man passed away. Do it the same way, but at a different spot. (*Frank takes a bible from a box and Eldon spots it.*) I guess we could....

ELDON: Don't throw that on the fire Frank! Jesus. (*Eldon takes the bible from Frank.*) Hey, remember? Colene Hammer came driving up and tried to get the old man's rifle. The octagon barrel .22?

FRANK: Yeah. The way she came driving up with all those wooden apple boxes in the back of her white Ford. Her small squinty eyes looking around the place. And that greasy apron she wears, big black spots on her dress. (*Frank laughs.*)

ELDON: Not that bad. Oh yeah, oh yeah. She said her cousin let her have the rifle. And all the time it was burning with the rest of dad's stuff. I thought she was going to scream when you told her if she wanted it, to go and get it. The fire melted the barrel into a 'U.' (*Pause.*) Where is Colene now? I thought she would show up by now.

FRANK: It's too early yet. The news hasn't gotten around. When the word does, she'll be stopping by. She'll come in that old Ford. Probably with a bunch of cardboard boxes in her trunk and plenty of her grandchildren to help her with her haul. (*Kermit enters. He is singing and carries a small paper sack. He sets the sack near the porch. He takes a bottle from the sack and drinks. Then he sets the bottle down and goes to the fire.*) It'll be just a matter of time. She'll come waddling into the yard like a fat duck to water . . . ah . . . I don't like. . . .(*Frank sees a figure.*) Hey! (*Pause.*) Who. . .Kermit? Is that you? (*Pause.*) Why don't you go into the house and stretch out?

KERMIT: Ma.

ELDON: Oh Christ. . .Yeah! (*Turns his back to Kermit.*) Kermit. You look tired.

KERMIT: Momma. . .oh. . .momma. . . .(*Stands at the fire.*)

FRANK: Come on Kermit. You need the rest. (*Grabs Kermit's arm.*) Let's go. (*He starts to lead Kermit, but Kermit breaks free and staggers.*)

KERMIT: No. . .No! I can do it by myself.

ELDON: Hey ringy! He's only trying to help you.

KERMIT: I can do it. . .I can do it! Fuck! (*He mumbles and staggers to the porch and sits. He takes out the bottle and drinks. Frank watches and Eldon takes the time to lift some of the pictures from the box and stick them inside his shirt.*)

ELDON: How is he? Is he going to get real ringy on us? (*Softly.*) Frank?

FRANK: Speak up! He'll be all right.

ELDON: Are you sure?

KERMIT: Yeah! Don't lose any sleep El'. I'm not going to die. I can hear you, even though I don't want to. . .goddamn it!

FRANK: But you'll have one hell of a hangover tomorrow. (*No reply from the two brothers.*) Christ. I remember drinking with him four years ago. He met me on a Friday night at the Long Horn. Denise took the kids and her mother to Bingo. (*Kermit gets up and walks to the brothers. He tries to hide his bottle on the way over.*)

KERMIT: You bet partner! What-yah, guys doing?

FRANK: I wasn't planning anything. Then I started drinking shots of whiskey and had beer chasers. Glad people told me otherwise I would've forgotten. Anyways, he came over and sat with me. And then it was park the car time. What was it you were drinking?

KERMIT: Mustn't tell. It was muscatel. (*He laughs and offers Frank a drink on the side.*)

FRANK: No thanks. When the Long Horn closed we got two cases of beer and a jug of wine and went to a house party, it was a house any way. We finished the beer and wine and I passed out.

KERMIT: Wussed out.

FRANK: Saturday afternoon we woke up, hot and sweaty in the truck. Bought another case of beer and went to Clem's bar, I think? Yeah. And we drank until Clem's closed. We drove around and finished off the case. I quit drinking Sunday and I think this guy went drinking until the next Sunday.

KERMIT: Hey, hey, hey Frank. You wussed out on me.

ELDON: See. This is what I mean.

KERMIT: Oh shit. You mad? Fuck! Good time, huh Frank? (*Pats Frank on the back and looks at Eldon. He goes back to the porch.*) My brother.

ELDON: Oh Christ. (*Pause.*) Now that mom is dead he'll. . . .

FRANK: No, no. . .it's up to him. One way or another, he'll decide for himself like I did. (*Pause.*)

ELDON: Are we going to have a feast after the funeral?

FRANK: Yeah. Claire said she would do it. The kids will help. Aunty Babbs, Joan and Ava said they would help too.

ELDON: When are we going to have the funeral?

FRANK: Wednesday.

ELDON: Why Wednesday? Hell, that's a four day wait. Hell that's two days after we're supposed to have the feast!

FRANK: I know.

ELDON: Kence just wants it on Wednesday cause he can make more money. Keeping her in storage like a piece of furniture.

FRANK: He's the only mortician in a 100 miles. Hell, I don't like him, but he is the only one, near by. (*Pause.*) Hey!

ELDON: What?

FRANK: Why don't we bury mom ourselves?

ELDON: You mean let Kence prepare the body and we dig the hole?

FRANK: I've been thinking. We don't need to put all those chemicals and perservatives in her body. Why preserve her dead body like she was a damn beet?

ELDON: I don't know Frank. . . .

FRANK: Well, I sure the hell do.

ELDON: It sounds well meant and all, but I think it would be breaking the law.

FRANK: Don't worry about the law. . . .

ELDON: Yeah but, Father Crane will be pissed if he doesn't get to pray over her.

FRANK: To hell with Crane. He was there when she died. He had a chance to sprinkle his water on her and pray over her.

ELDON: If you think about it that way. . . .

FRANK: Remember when I used to work for Kence Senior? He told me the secret for funerals El'. You want to know what they are? One- you need a dead body. Two- a hole in the ground. Three- transportation to get the body to the hole in the ground. Four- start a bank account.

ELDON: No. . .uh–huh. . .no. . .no. . . .

FRANK: Don't worry. I'll take care of you. (*Pause.*) We have a right to do this. Even Kermit.

ELDON: Not that drunk.

FRANK: We're all family.

ELDON: But what about the relatives?

FRANK: Mom was the last of her family. We have to stick together and ride this one out. We're all the family she has left. The others, they'll know.

ELDON: Frank... Frank.... (*Pause.*) You're just... you're really serious about this.

FRANK: Damn right I am.

ELDON: I thought you were just joking.

FRANK: No. And I'm not doing it because I'm trying to get out of Kence's fee. We'll give him his money when we're finished. (*Pause.*) I want us to bury her. Not a stranger with his strange ways.

ELDON: How will we do it?

FRANK: She's always talked about being buried in the traditional way, remember?

ELDON: Yeah? Where are we going to start shoveling?

FRANK: Nooo... Eldon, no, not their way, our traditional way. Not buried in the ground. Bury her with the wind, in a tree.

ELDON: What about her decaying smell in the wind?

FRANK: If you're worried about the smell, we can burn the body after the funeral. Just like in the old days, no one will find it. We can find an old tree and place dry wood around it and set them on fire.

ELDON: Then, why don't we just have her cremated? I'll pay for part of the cost.

FRANK: You're not listening. It isn't the money that's important. Way back when, it was the responsibility of the family to bury their own.

ELDON: That was a long time ago. Two or three hundred years ago. It isn't right.

FRANK: Not right who, Eldon? Us, Eldon? This way, her grave won't be disturbed. They uncover a bunch of unmarked graves and take the bodies out and that isn't right. And in a few more years, who knows? Some scientist will come along and discover mom's body and take it off to some college, or university. Her skull sitting on a little wood box under glass. Her bones sawed up, spine and all, like beef ribs. Then, they'll put them under a

microscope. Is that right? I sure the hell don't thing so. And I'm not go-
ing to allow it to happen. (*Pause.*) Goddamn it El'. (*Pause.*)

ELDON: Well, do you really know how to bury her in the traditional way?
I don't recall of having heard of anybody doing it recently. I don't know
of anyone who has done it, or remembers seeing it. And if nobody knows
how to do it, I don't want to mess with it.

FRANK: You don't huh? I remember grandma telling us how they used
to do it. And I remember a little of what grandpa told me.

ELDON: Yeah? Do you know enough about it so we can do it right?

FRANK: Grandma told me how to do it. And I know she told it to you
and Kermit when she used to babysit us. If we try to do it right, and do,
do it right. We'll tell our kids about it. And they'll tell their kids. We
can keep it going just like grandpa and grandma did with us.

ELDON: But what about the law? Her will? And if we're not caught by
the cops we still have Kence to settle with. And I don't want to mess
with that guy.

FRANK: I've seen the will.

ELDON: How did you see it?

FRANK: In her last couple of weeks, she called me to her house and asked
me to be with her. That's when she made her will out. Kence was there too.

ELDON: Why didn't mom call me?

FRANK: I don't know. Mom probably didn't want to bother you.

ELDON: I would have come if somebody would have told me. They call-
ed me for everything else. Christ! What the hell was Kence doing there?
I'm her own son.

FRANK: Anyway! In her will she was going to request to be buried near
the place she grew up at. She wanted to be buried in the traditional way.
And Kence told her it wasn't possible. He knew where she wanted to
be buried at, but he didn't know how to perform it. He didn't know
how to do it. And he suggested she go with the American traditional
funeral. (*Pause.*)

ELDON: Well, why didn't you say something then, Frank? Huh?

FRANK: Not in front of Kence; he would have really put the blocks to
us before we even had a chance.

ELDON: It just doesn't seem right. We could get caught.

FRANK: Who's going to know, huh?

ELDON: Someone will see us and tell. Maybe one of mom's friends. . . .

FRANK: They won't tell. I'll explain it to them. I'll put the will in the Tribal newspaper if you want me to. Will and all, El', mom didn't like the white man's funeral. She said, all it has to do with, is money, and nothing else. You can't even cry without the priest's permission. (*Kermit slowly staggers to them.*) If you decide no, we can't do it. You're the second to the oldest.

ELDON: If you can't do it without me. . .I'm a member of the family now, huh? Okay, I'll go along with you. And we'll even take Kermit with us. But we have to keep this to ourselves. I don't want this going through the moccasin telegraph.

FRANK: It'll go through the moccasin telegraph. By the time it gets around the res. it'll be too late for Kence and cops to do anything.

ELDON: It sounds slick. . . .

KERMIT: What's up? (*Tries to place his hand on Frank's shoulder.*)

FRANK: Kermit. We've decided to bury mom ourselves. What do you think?

KERMIT: Hell yes! Let's do-er! (*He nearly walks into the fire, but is saved by Frank.*)

ELDON: Chh. . .Christ! He's not even in walking condition. Frank, if we get caught it'll be because of him. He's lost his mud. He hasn't cared about mom. He's lived off of her. Now he wants to help us steal her from the morgue because you've come up with this idea.

KERMIT: What? Steal momma?

FRANK: Hold on now Eldon. He has the right to be a part of this too. You wouldn't like to bury mom yourself?

KERMIT: Yeah, you tightass.

ELDON: Shut up.

FRANK: I want us to do the burying because that's the way we've always done things. By ourselves and together. We didn't get to bury dad, but now we've got a chance to bury mom ourselves.

KERMIT: What's this shit about stealing mom-ma?

FRANK: We're going to take mom from the mortician and bury her ourselves. Are you in?

KERMIT: Shit-yeah! (*He falls and Franks tries to catch him.*)

ELDON: Goddamn it!

FRANK: Don't be afraid of Jack Kence. I'll handle him.

ELDON: Like you did at mom's will? I'm not afraid of him. Who said I was?

KERMIT: Fuck you. You're afraid of him because he has money. I'm not. I'm like Frank.

ELDON: Shut up you drunk. (*He goes to Kermit and pushes him.*)

FRANK: Easy Eldon. I know Kence has money and a lot of connections, but he has our mother.

KERMIT: Yeah.

FRANK: We're going to get her back. When mom died, no one asked me what I wanted. Kence just came in and took her without permission.

ELDON: Yes, but he has a right Frank. He's a mortician. The county coroner. It's his job.

FRANK: It's our job Eldon. And the thing is we don't get paid for doing it.

KERMIT: That's right. We can't let the son of a bitch do our job for us.

ELDON: What if he calls the cops on us? Huh? Or even the FBI? We could be up shit creek without a paddle. And if we go to jail? Hell, the Pen! What happens to my family?

KERMIT: They'll be better off.

ELDON: Shut up Kermit! You don't have a wife and kids to worry about. I do. And you have kids too, Frank. What happens to them? How are we going to support them from prison?

FRANK: We won't get caught El'. Your problem is you're always thinking like one of them. So what if Kence has connections with the cops. That's the risk we have to take.

ELDON: Okay.

KERMIT: You're damned right. I'm behind you one hundred per-cent. (*He goes into a fast grass dance and does a few steps and nearly falls over into the fire, but is saved by Frank.*)

FRANK: We're not cooking frybread. If you burn yourself up you aren't going to be worth shit to us.

ELDON: You're not as it is now.

KERMIT: Sure I am. I can keep watch for you guys. No problem.

FRANK: Okay. Let's get started.

ELDON: What about the fire? (*Eldon picks up some of the boxes and turns his back to his brothers.*)

FRANK: We'll shovel dirt on it. (*Eldon walks off.*)

ELDON: One big chief and a damn drunken Indian.

FRANK: What?

KERMIT: Damn right. (*Kermit attacks the fire and Frank helps him toss dirt onto the fire. Blackout. End of Scene Two.*)

Scene Three

(*Frank and Eldon hide behind and run to several objects before they reach the funeral home. They enter the funeral home and Frank leads Eldon to the surgical room. Kermit is slowly following his brothers. Two slabs are in the middle of the room. A surgical tray is at the side of each slab. A large sink is on one side of the wall. The other wall is lined with glass and wood cabinets. Each cabinet contains surgical equipment. Bodies lie on each slab. The bodies are covered with sheets large enough to hang to the floor of the 'gurneys' or 'slabs.' The brothers are carrying flashlights.*)

ELDON: God it smells in here. What is that smell, Frank?

FRANK: Death and all its causes. (*Eldon's light shines on the bodies.*)

ELDON: Hey! There are two of them. How do we know which one of them is mom?

FRANK: You do the one of the right and I'll do the left. (*Kermit enters the room. He is humming the theme song from a popular spy series. The two brothers go to the bodies. Kermit goes to Eldon. Frank is first in pulling back the sheet.*)

FRANK: I found her. I found mom. (*Eldon pulls back the sheet and he looks at Frank. Frank shakes his head, 'no.' And then Eldon looks at the body.*)

ELDON: Ohhh...my...god....

KERMIT: What's up El'? Can't handle it, aaye? (*Kermit looks at the body and becomes sick.*) Ohhh....

FRANK: Hold on. Hang on to it. (*Eldon gets sick. Frank grabs Eldon and Kermit and takes them to the sink. Frank goes back to the slab and examines the body. He finds a foot tab.*) Jesus. It's uncle Joe Yellow Foote and half his face is gone. (*Kermit and Eldon take turns vomiting into the sink. Frank reads the foot tag.*) Accident victim: Hit and run. Identification: Joseph Alvin Yellow Foote, Senior. Vagrant.

ELDON: God, it made me sick. Let's take the body and go.

FRANK: You're right Eldon. Kermit? Can you make it back to the pickup by yourself?

KERMIT: Who...who...who hit me? (*He is on his hands and knees rocking back and forth. Slobber dangles from his mouth and touches the floor. He slumps to the floor.*) Son of a bitch! Who hit me goddamn it! Come on! I'll take you all on....

FRANK: Better help him out to the truck El'. He won't make it by himself.

ELDON: Are you going to carry mom by yourself?

FRANK: No. But he needs help.

KERMIT: Float like a butterfly...sing like a bee...grasshopper.

ELDON: We'll get caught. I know it.

FRANK: El'. Listen to me. You help Kermit get back to the truck and I'll clean up this mess. Then come back and help me. (*Frank walks back to Kermit and helps Kermit to his feet.*)

KERMIT: Bring them on...bring them all on. ...

ELDON: All right, all right, I'll do it.

KERMIT: Frank, Frank? We'll take them all on. ...

FRANK: Right Kermit. (*They begin to walk to the door.*)

KERMIT: Oh...Christ! Mom-ma!

FRANK: Hurry up El'. Just do it. Be sure to come back and help me. (*Eldon finds a place to grab Kermit and leads him out the door. Frank starts a search for paper towels. He finds them and wets them in the sink. He starts to wipe the floor where Kermit was and then the sink. He looks for a garbage can. He finds one, but; it is filled. He steps on the pedal of another can and the lid opens. Frank crams the paper towels into the can. The can is a disposal can for dead organs and tissue. Frank nearly vomits. He washes his hands and is faced again with the task of disposing of the the paper towels. He wads them up and puts them in his shirt pocket. He glances around the room and does a quick 'go over' of the room, checks the floor, and then the two slabs. He goes over to his mother and gently removes the sheet from her face.*) Ma. I don't... (*He gently covers her face.*) I don't know if I can live without you. You've always given me your support. Helped me out when I needed it. My whole family loves you. We're all going to miss you. (*Eldon enters. He stops and watches.*) You've worked hard all your life mom. And now you suffer no pain. Thank you for being our mother. It'll be really tough without you in this world. We'll try. And we'll always remember you. Damn. I don't know if I can carry this whole family mom. Please help me find a way to do it. . .or to let go. (*Pause.*) We should all be going and just let go.

ELDON: Frank? (*Crosses to Frank.*) Frank? (*Goes to Joe's body.*)

FRANK: Goodbye uncle Joe. (*Pause.*) What is it?

ELDON: There's a security cop. Are you all right?

FRANK: Yeah.

ELDON: Well. There's a security cop. I thought he saw me and Kermit. So I headed down the alley.

FRANK: Where's Kermit.

ELDON: I put him in a garbage bin. We'll get him later.

FRANK: Damn.

ELDON: He'll be all right. He doesn't even know what's going on. When I put him in he gave me his wallet. Let's get mom. (*They both go to the body and pick it up. A light shines under the door.*)

FRANK: Oh-oh! Someone's coming El'.

ELDON: You take her. (*He drops his end of the body. Frank hangs onto his end of the body.*)

FRANK: What the hell are you doing El'? Just pick her up and we'll get her back on the slab and hide. (*They do and hide. The door opens and a ray of light sweeps the room. Frank hides behind a cabinet. Eldon hides along side the body of Joe, covering himself with Joe's sheet. The light stops and the door closes.*) El' . . .El'? I think it's okay. Let's go. Where are you?

ELDON: Ohhh. . .man. (*He climbs out from under the sheet. Frank crosses to him.*)

FRANK: Don't feel bad. I would have done the same thing.

ELDON: Okay. I'm sorry I dropped mom. I want to go now. I don't want to hang around here.

FRANK: You're not the only one. We'll have to wait a bit.

ELDON: Why? The guard is gone. Don't know why you would need a guard at a funeral home any way.

FRANK: Somebody might steal something.

ELDON: Oh Christ.

FRANK: Really. There are a lot of expensive things around here. When I was working here somebody stole some clothes.

ELDON: Clothes?

FRANK: Yeah. Kence has clothes here that zip up the back. It makes it easier for him to dress the body.

ELDON: Who stole them?

FRANK: Remember that one year all the winos around town looked real sharp?

ELDON: Jesus. How could they? Let's go. (*Frank goes to the door and looks out. Eldon sniffs himself.*)

FRANK: It looks okay, but let's wait for a bit more. He was probably making his rounds. (*Crosses to Eldon.*)

ELDON: Do I stink?

FRANK: Sometimes, but not now. You're okay.

ELDON: Okay, but I want to get cleaned up before we have the funeral. I'll get a star quilt. We're not going to bury mom in this.

FRANK: (*Crosses to door and checks.*) All right. (*Crosses back to Eldon.*) It's okay. Ready? (*Picks up one end of the body and Eldon the other.*)

ELDON: Frank? Are you scared?

FRANK: Yeah. Let's take mom and make some tracks. (*They carry the body out. They stop on the way and pick Kermit up. They carry Kermit and the mother in the blanket. Blackout. End of Scene Three.*)

Scene Four

TIME: It is very early morning. The next day.
PLACE: It is five miles from town. Near the river
and a clearing of a meadow.

(*There is a human mound. It is Kermit and the body. Kermit stirs and rolls off
the body. He rolls near a small fire. He shakes a little from the morning cold.
Then he reaches out to wrap a blanket around himself. The blanket isn't there.
He slowly wakes up. He rests himself on his elbows and tries to refocus his eyes.
He sees his mother with her blanket.*)

KERMIT: Damn it's chilly. (*Pause.*) Did you go to the softball tournament
too? I didn't see you. You probably seen me. (*No reply.*) I sure am
cold. . .and lonesome. (*Leans towards her.*) You know, hey? You know.
You have a blanket. And I don't have any. Brrr. . .And I suppose you're
cold too. (*He touches her.*) Damn. . .Damn! You're real cold. . .freezing.
(*Touches himself.*) Hey! Hey. . .there partner. I tell you what. You share
your blanket with me. I'll be good. (*No reply.*) Don't worry. Don't worry
honey. I won't hurt you even if you don't want to share your blanket.
(*No reply.*) Don't be stuck up. I'll even let you sleep near the fire. Bee. . .be,
be sure you don't burn yourself from the sparks. (*No relpy.*) Come on.
Share your blanket. Come on. . .come. . .come on. I'm cold. And I know
you're freezing to death. (*He begins to pull at the blanket.*) Don't be a tight
ass. Come on baby. Share with me. (*Eldon and Frank enter.*) Baby. . .darlin'.
Baby cakes?

ELDON: And, after I went home and showered, I guess the cops called
while I was showering up. My wife told them I was sleeping and. . . .

KERMIT: Oh baby. Ohhh. . .baby, baby, sweet baby cakes. . . . (*He car-
resses the shoulder of the mother.*)

ELDON: What the hell is he doing? I thought he was passed out.

FRANK: How the hell do I know.

KERMIT: Yeah. Oooh. . .baby. (*He uses his other hand to caress.*)

ELDON: Oh shit! (*Runs over and kicks Kermit away.*)

KERMIT: Oww. . .Fuck!

ELDON: Frank, you see what he was doing?

FRANK: Yeah.

KERMIT: I wasn't doing anything wrong. Fuck. I was doing it with love.

ELDON: I thought you said if we left him alone, passed out, he wouldn't do anything. It would be all right.

FRANK: I was wrong.

ELDON: Do something then Frank!

FRANK: What? What do you want me to do Eldon?

KERMIT: It's just a girl. Christ. Eldon fucking freaks out on everything. Shit!

ELDON: A girl? You don't know, do you? Frank. He doesn't even know.

FRANK: He's been drinking Eldon. He just must be coming out of it.

ELDON: All right Frank. A girl huh? Come here. (*Grabs Kermit and pulls him near the mother's face.*) It's mom, Kermit. It's your mother. (*Kermit looks at the face.*)

FRANK: Kermit?

KERMIT: Ohhh. . .god. . .damn. . . . (*He crawls away from the body. He scratches at the ground.*) Damn. . .damn. . .it. . . .

ELDON: I had to Frank. And you Frank, you are going to have to stop taking care of him. You bought him that wine tonight. He has to live down whatever he does.

FRANK: I know. Yeah. (*Kermit takes a bottle from his pocket and tries to open it. He uses his teeth to pry the cap off and can't do it. He picks up a twig and tries to use that to get the cap off and can't.*)

KERMIT: I can't do it. (*No reply.*) One of you guys. . .Hey! (*No reply.*) One of you guys open this for me. Please. (*He tries again to open the bottle.*) Help me. Goddamn it! Frank. Help me. I'll get sick. (*Frank starts to walk to Kermit but is stopped by Eldon.*) I. . .I. . .I need your help. (*Eldon comes to Kermit. He takes the bottle from Kermit's shaking hands and opens the bottle.*) Thank you Eldon. I love you for this. Give it to me. (*Eldon slowly turns the bottle upside down and pours out the liquid.*) What. . .What. . .What the fuck are you doing? (*He charges Eldon like a dog and tries to stop Eldon. Eldon holds him off with one hand and with the other continues to pour.*) Fuck. Frank. No!

No! Let me go. Goddamn you Eldon! Stop. Frank...Frank! Stop him! You guys...Hey! (*Kermit tries to stop the brothers.*) Frank! Damn you guys! No! (*The bottle is emptied. Frank slowly releases Kermit. Eldon lets the bottle drop. He looks at Kermit and tries to help him up. Kermit spits on him.*) Fuck you Eldon! Why the fuck did you guys do that? Huh?

ELDON: I had to Kermit. (*Eldon crosses to Kermit and tries to hug him. Kermit fights Eldon off and gets away from Frank.*)

KERMIT: Keep away from me.

FRANK: Come on you guys. Knock it off.

KERMIT: Why the hell did you have to do that? Huh?

ELDON: Because you were drunk. I don't want my little brother to be a drunk.

KERMIT: You're an apple, red on the outside, white on the...Hell! You're white all over, in and out. You're a whiteman. We should cut you out.

ELDON: What? No...I'm your brother.

FRANK: Don't say any more you two.

KERMIT: You know what mom used to say Eldon, huh? She used to say how she raised two Indin' sons and one businessman.

ELDON: That's a lie.

KERMIT: She said one loves celebrations, one loves hunting and building things and the other one loves money.

ELDON: She didn't mean it that way Kermit. That's not true.

KERMIT: You're a whiteman, Eldon. I hate to see one of my older brothers turn into a whiteman. You dress like Jack Kence, you even smell like him.

ELDON: Stop it Kermit.

KERMIT: Mr. Chamber of Commerce. Only Indin' there. Yeah. And you're such a big wheel. You and your stink smokeshack. Indins' around here are laughing at you behind your back.

ELDON: I don't give a shit about that.

KERMIT: That's probably why you wanted all of mom's things. So you could sell them at your smokeshack.

ELDON: No. It was for my girls. They. . . .

KERMIT: Mr. Businessman. Last Thanksgiving. When you put that big cardboard cut out around your smokeshack, the trailer. No one else but you. Ohhh...shit. (*Laughs.*) All the places I've been. All the Indin' people I know. You're the only one who celebrates Thanksgiving, the coming of the whiteman. But then again, it's like welcoming your true brothers, huh? Isn't it. You break your ass recognizing them, but you sure as shit can't recognize me when you see me on the street, can you?

ELDON: I've always come to help.

FRANK: Don't be talking about these things now Kermit.

KERMIT: Why not? Now's as good a time as any. He'll leave and forget all about us. Ignore us when he sees us because we're Indins' and he's not.

ELDON: I only ignored you one time Kermit! One time! And that's because you were sitting on the steps of the Grant Hotel. You've probably forgotten that...I bet you don't even remember. (*Pause.*) You had puked all over yourself and didn't know it. Pee'd your pants your hair was greasy and matted and you didn't know it. You were bumming people who were coming and going into the hotel. You were mumbling away. (*Pause.*) The cops wanted to take you in. They stopped at the smokeshack and told me, but I talked with them and told them, promised them, I would take you to my home and clean you up. And when I pulled up and parked my car. You were mumbling my name, 'Eldon,' 'Eldon.' I walked over to you and you didn't even hear me when I called your name. You didn't even recognize my voice. You didn't recognize me period. I felt so bad for you. I picked you up and took you to my house and cleaned you up. And then, I...I cried. (*Pause.*) Ever since that time I told myself. I promised myself. If I ever saw you drunk like that again. I wouldn't recognize you. It would be easier for me if you were some other wino, but you're my brother. (*Pause.*) It is true Kermit. I didn't recognize you. And there were times I didn't want to recognize Frank and Dad. All three of you were drunk. What hurts me the most, you all three treated me like drunks, not a brother. Just because, I didn't drink with you guys, didn't mean I was too good. It meant I was sober. (*Pause.*) The next time Kermit...I will disown you.

KERMIT: See...See! Too fucking good!

FRANK: I would've done the same thing Kermit.

KERMIT: No You wouldn't...no...Frank. You're my brother. Not like this guy.

ELDON: Damn you. (*Charges Kermit.*)

FRANK: Don't Eldon.

KERMIT: You want to fight, huh? (*Struggles getting to his feet.*) I'll kick your fucking ass. Come on. You and the big son of a bitch Frank. Both of you, come on!

FRANK: Knock it off Kermit!

KERMIT: You're not so fucking good as you act Frank.

FRANK: Shut up Kermit!

KERMIT: But first I'm going to knock the shit out of this bastard. Yeah. Both of you had no problems getting rid of mom's stuff. You're both alike.

FRANK: You'd better settle down.

KERMIT: I don't have to. Damn it! Come on and fight! (*He slaps Eldon. Eldon doesn't do anything. Kermit tries to dance around like a boxer. He tries to slap Eldon again, but Eldon grabs his arm and pulls Kermit to him and holds him. Kermit tries to break free.*) Damn you! You fucking ass! Let me go. . . I can take care of. . .of myself. (*Kermit stops struggling. Eldon loosens his hold. There is a sound of a car. Frank crosses to the brothers and touches them. The sound of the car becomes louder.*)

ELDON: What?

FRANK: Listen. It's a car.

ELDON: Who can it be? Maybe it's just a farmer.

FRANK: I don't know. Did you close the fence gate?

ELDON: I think so.

FRANK: You better go check and see. (*Eldon begins to exit.*) Wait! We don't have time.

ELDON: What do we do?

FRANK: We have to hide mom.

ELDON: Let's cover her up. (*They cover her with the blanket.*)

FRANK: It won't work.

ELDON: What if one of us lies down and pretends we're sleeping. . . . (*They look at Kermit.*)

KERMIT: Oh. . .no. . .no!

FRANK: Come on Kermit. You have to. Just this one time.

ELDON: If you do it, we don't have to come up with a good excuse. . . .

KERMIT: No. . .Ah. . .shit. . . . (*He starts to go to his knees. Eldon removes the blanket from their mother's body. Kermit lies on top of the mother and they cover them. Jack Kence enters.*)

FRANK: Be quiet Kermit.

JACK: Good morning.

FRANK: Hello Jack.

ELDON: Uh. . .Hi Jack.

JACK: Goddamn, it's chilly this morning. What're you boys doing out here so early?

ELDON: We. . .We're gathering a few things for the feast. You know, tea, meat. . . .

JACK: Well, you guys shouldn't be spotlighting. It's illegal. Hard to do without any rifles.

ELDON: Jack. . .That's because we're not allowed to use rifles, traditionally. We use our cars.

JACK: Uh-huh.

FRANK: Calm down Eldon. What're you doing here Jack?

JACK: I have one hell of a mess on my hands Frank. You see. I got a phone call from my security man. It's kind of embarrassing. He said Elva Rose's body is missing. Said he saw your pick-up outside of my place last night. Well, I kinda figured you might know (*pause*) where your mom's body is at.

ELDON: By golly, we don't know what the hell you're talking about Jack.

JACK: Oh. I see. (*Notices the body.*) What's this over here?

ELDON: It's our baby brother. He's asleep.

JACK: Well, what's he laying on. (*Crosses to the body.*) Let's take a look.

ELDON: Oh shit, oh shit. . . . (*He begins to take off but is stopped by Frank.*)

JACK: Kermit? Come on kid. Get up. (*Eldon crosses over to Jack and stops Jack from touching the body.*)

ELDON: I said, it was our baby brother Jack.

JACK: But this blanket is familiar. (*Pulls on the blanket and then Kermit.*) Get up kid. (*Rolls Kermit off the body.*) Oh Christ. Have you guys lost your marbles? (*Jack examines the body.*) Didn't really damage anything.

ELDON: Sorry Jack. . . .

JACK: Sorry shit! Eldon. Help me take this back to my car.

FRANK: Take your hands off our mother Jack.

JACK: Look. This is getting really sick. Now help me take your mother back to my place, and we'll forget all about this. Eldon.

ELDON: I can't.

JACK: Why not?

KERMIT: Why should he? You're just a whiteman.

JACK: Lookit now! I know this is a difficult time. I have a job to do. Now help me out and we can all go home and forget this happened. (*No response.*) I'm not in a great mood guys. I don't want to be out here all damn morning long, let's go. (*No response.*) Frank be reasonable. All right. Eldon. Give me a hand here. I'm taking this body back with me. (*No response.*) You fella's don't seem to understand this. We seem to have a hell of a time communicating like normal people. She belongs to me, mine, and I still have a lot of work to do. I have to do some more preparations, dress her up and I'm backed up at the home. The sooner I can get this one done, I can do the next one. Now come on El'. (*Eldon moves forward then stops.*)

ELDON: I can't Jack. My brothers and I have decided she's going to stay with us.

JACK: What?

FRANK: That's right Jack. Our mother is staying with us.

JACK: All the times you used to work with my father, Frank. I thought you were more reasonable than this.

FRANK: I am Jack.

JACK: Not as far as I can see.

KERMIT: Then you must be white and blind.

JACK: Be quiet kid. You guys can get into a lot of trouble for this. I'm not joking. I hate to see it happen.

FRANK: That's the chance we're willing to take.

JACK: I came here without notifying the police where I was going. The cops, both Tribal and White, are patrolling all around town and the surrounding area looking for your lost mother.

KERMIT: Did you tell them what she was wearing hey?

JACK: Kermit. I've always heard you were a little drunken smart ass. But I didn't think it was this bad.

KERMIT: Makes you the dumb ass on the bottom of the totem pole, doesn't it.

JACK: Goddamn. If you guys don't give me some damn good reasons in the next few minutes. I'll have to go back to my car and call the cops out here. You can save us all a lot of trouble if you can give me a hand and take your mother's body back to my car and I'll take it back with me.

KERMIT: Do it yourself. We don't work for you.

JACK: It looks like I might have to do that. (*Jack goes to the body and starts to lift it. Eldon walks over and grabs his arm.*) Let go, damn you!

ELDON: No. Jack. We can't let you do this.

JACK: You shouldn't do this Eldon. You, of all people, know better. This is mine. I'm taking your mother back with me.

FRANK: Our mother is staying with us.

JACK: You know Eldon. I remember a young man coming up, working very hard to succeed in business, and making it, the first Indian to make the Chamber of Commerce. Now, to lose it all on one bad move. I know you must have had one hell of a battle with the bottle. . . .

ELDON: Damn it! Jack. I never have drank. I don't drink now. I never had no damn battle with any damn bottle. None of you knows me.

FRANK: I think you'd better leave Jack.

JACK: What the hell for?

FRANK: We're going to bury mom ourselves.

JACK: You are? Why?

FRANK: We know what type of funeral she wanted.

JACK: And what kind is that Frank, huh? What kind?

FRANK: One that isn't bought and paid for. That doesn't come out from any show-case. She always wanted to be buried the Indin' way.

JACK: What do you think I would've done? Put her in a pine box and leave her on the side of a hill, unburied?

FRANK: They don't do that any more, or do they?

JACK: You and your brothers are going to perform the funeral. You're the priest, he's the undertaker and Kermit is the grave digger?

FRANK: And notice, too, we are all family. We know each other.

JACK: We have laws, health codes, state and federal. It isn't that simple.

FRANK: It was at one time. Just like dying was. Only you didn't have to pay anybody back then. And you had the time to say goodbye to the one you loved. You didn't have to rush because the priest had an appointment, like a pot-luck. And, our way means, we don't have to worry about the price of a hearse, or coffin, just the loss of the one we love.

JACK: You don't want your mom-ma buried like the way white people do? And I'm so evil for that? You have to do better than that Frank. A whole lot better. I've buried a lot of white people and your people in my day. They all have on thing in common, after a certain amount of time, they rot and they're forgotten.

FRANK: And, I'm not going to let that happen.

JACK: But not with this body.

FRANK: You want a body Jack? Here. Here's some money. (*Takes out some bills from his pocket and then gives them to Jack.*) This should take care of all the costs. And you want a body? Here. Take this one. (*Pushes Eldon to Jack.*) Or this one. Take this guy. (*Pushes Kermit.*)

JACK: Oh Christ.

FRANK: You want a body. Take one of these guys, or hell, take me. You're going to get one of us sooner, or later.

JACK: All right. Damn it. You've had your fun. You tell me one thing. What mandate of heaven do you have that the rest of us don't? You seem to have taken all the weight and secrets of the world on your shoulders. (*He walks up to Frank and puts the bills into Frank's pocket.*) Go ahead.

FRANK: It's easy, my beliefs. When I say them, I mean them.

JACK: I'm getting tired and it's getting chillier. I'm thinking really seriously about getting the cops out here.

FRANK: You do that! You go ahead. I don't care what you do to us after this funeral. Just don't try to stop us from having this funeral. I'm willing to sacrifice whatever I have to, Jack. Having this woman as a mother was a great gift. And now we're returning her back to her god. . . her family. . .her relations. . .those dead. (*Pause.*) We have an old woman to bury now, Jack. You can stay and watch, or get into your car and drive off. It's a threat, or an offer. Seriously, hey, it is serious, as serious as burying our mother. Now, we have a funeral to start, Jack. And you're invited if you want to attend.

JACK: Frank. You can have your little funeral. Don't even bother to pay me. Listen to me though, this is my threat, warning or whatever the hell you want to call it. Don't you, or your brothers ever cross me again. This is the last time and the first time it happens. I don't know if I can completely forget this. You guys sure the hell hope I do. (*He begins to walk away.*) I provide a service for people. You remember that. A service and what they pay me for that service doesn't mean a thing. I do the work most people can't. (*Pause.*) Enjoy your services. (*Starts to leave.*) For Christ's-sake.

ELDON: Goodbye Jack. (*Turns to Frank.*) Do you think he'll tell the cops?

FRANK: Wait.

ELDON: We sure the hell did show him though, huh? We'd better hurry up and start the funeral. If he tells the police we won't have one.

FRANK: Wait a minute El'. (*Car engine starts.*) I'm going to be right back.

ELDON: Maybe. . .You're not running out on us, are you?

FRANK: I said I'll be right back. (*Frank exits.*)

ELDON: Pretty shaky ground, huh Kermit? Kermit? Hey, Kermit. What's wrong with you?

KERMIT: You don't know what's wrong? Christ. It's what I did to mom. I do all kinds of things, but I can never remember them.

ELDON: Yeah. I know.

KERMIT: What's that? (*Sound of truck leaving.*)

ELDON: That's Frank.

KERMIT: What's he going to do?

ELDON: I don't know.

KERMIT: Well, you still mad at me?

ELDON: Do you really want to know? (*Pause.*) You know Kermit, when you're sober. I don't mind having you around. I like your company. When you're drunk, you can be a pain in the ass. You're the last person I want to have around me. Never knew anyone I wanted to hurt as much as you. I don't know what I feel like, now. Too much has happened. (*Pause.*) I don't know.

KERMIT: What about mom?

ELDON: What about her? I mean, she was really worried about you. She always thought you might accidentally get run over, freeze to death, get hit   by a train. Sometimes she just couldn't have helped. It happened to uncle Joe.

KERMIT: He wasn't really our uncle.

ELDON: We claimed him.

KERMIT: Do you claim me? Tell me the truth?

ELDON: You're my brother through blood. I could disown you. I don't know any more. Blood and whiskey are two different things.

KERMIT: Ach-noc-shaw-luke.

ELDON: What the hell does that mean?

KERMIT: It's Klingon. You know. . .your girls watch it. Live long and prosper.

ELDON: All this time, I thought. . .Hey. Why don't you and I learn to speak Assiniboine. We can find someone to help us.

KERMIT: Just you and me, huh? I don't know. What if I bring someone else with me?

ELDON: No. This is something we can do ourselves, or we don't do it. (*Frank enters.*)

FRANK: Ready? (*He carries a sack.*)

KERMIT: Where'd you go?

FRANK: I used my pick-up to block the road. Now no one can get in. Where's your quilt El'?

ELDON: Oh yeah. Forgot. Be right back. (*He exits.*)

KERMIT: What's in the sack?

FRANK: Some things for mom. Tobacco, pemmican, a knife.

KERMIT: Nothing from K-Mart huh? (*Pause.*) You know. I didn't think I'd be sober for this funeral.

FRANK: Yeah. Help me get some wood around the tree. (*They start gathering wood.*)

KERMIT: Frank? I didn't do anything that bad, huh?

FRANK: Put the wood around the tree near the trunk. (*Kermit does.*) I didn't like the things you said to Eldon. He was all bent out of shape since we started this thing. I was too.

KERMIT: Pretty bad, huh?

FRANK: If I said I wanted to pound the shit out of you it'udd give you a reason to get drunk. If I don't, I would be lying. (*Stops gathering wood.*) What I was going to talk to you about, was this. I need you sober. I don't want you around me when you're drunk. I won't help you. I'm not mom. I won't be carrying this family all the time. I know that now. You have to decide what you want. I already have. Dad was afraid to die. He was alone. He thought he was alone. When I was drinking I thought I was alone. I was afraid of everything. Then I quit, I found others who are like me. I wasn't afraid of living, like you are now. Don't be. There are people here, among our people, who can help you, pray for you. I'll help you, sober, and only sober. It can be done Kermit.

KERMIT: Oh. (*Pause.*) I just don't know how to live right now. I'll learn. (*Pause.*) Might as well learn to talk too while I'm at it. (*Eldon enters.*)

ELDON: Got it.

FRANK: You and Kermit roll mom up in it. (*Eldon spreads the blanket out and he and Kermit roll her up in it like rolling a cigarette. Frank places more wood around the tree.*)

ELDON: Done.

FRANK: Now we'll put her in the tree. El'. You take her shoulders, that end. And Kermit, you take a stick and push back the branches when we put her in it. (*They place the body into the tree. Frank sets the sack on top of the mother. He takes a braid of sweet grass from the back of his pocket.*) Before I light this, I want you to pray.

KERMIT: I hate to interupt you brother. Is there any special prayer we should say?

FRANK: Yeah. Your own. (*He lights the sweet grass. Makes a circle around the brothers and himself.*)

KERMIT: Now what hey?

FRANK: I don't know. This is all I can remember.

ELDON: We should pray again, huh? The Lord's prayer can be for mom, as well for white people.

FRANK: (*Awkwardly makes the sign of the cross.*) Our father, who are in heaven, hello it be thy name. Thy kingdom come. . .Thy kingdom come. . . .

KERMIT: Does it have to be done.

FRANK: Does it have to be done on earth as it is in heaven. Give us our day and our daily. . .our daily. . . .

KERMIT: Daily fry bread.

FRANK: Daily fry bread. And forgive us our sins as we forgive those who have. . .those who have. . . .

KERMIT: Those who have thrashed ass against us.

FRANK: Yeah. Those who have thrashed ass against us. Lead us not into temptation o' Lord, but deliver us from. . .from. . .from. . . .

KERMIT: Lies. Thank you Kermit. (*Kermit farts.*)

KERMIT: You're welcome.

ELDON: Oh heavenly father. These two men here are my brothers. We've come to bury our mother. She was a good woman. In all this world you have given us great things. Each other, and most importantly, this woman. We thank you. Amen.

KERMIT: Is this all?

FRANK: I guess it is. I've got stuff to make torches back at my truck. Let's go.

KERMIT: You guys go ahead. I want to think about some things.

FRANK: Sure. Come on El'. (*They exit.*)

KERMIT: Go on my son, go and climb a ladder, go my son, get an edu. . . (*Stops singing.*) Frank? (*Looks to where his brothers have gone.*) Frank? (*He looks up at the body.*) You're probably wondering why I called you here. . . (*He laughs and starts to walk away and nearly trips.*) Ma? Ma! Don't do this. . .please. . .I. . .I. . .I don't know what to do. I don't know. I thought I'd know what to do. Honest I really did. (*Pause.*) Ma! (*Softly to himself.*) Mom-ma I. . . (*He goes to where Frank was standing and picks up the burning braid of sweet grass and tries to breathe in the smoke and then he lets the braid drop.*) Damn. (*He stands and looks at the body.*) Ma. I don't know what to say. I always thought I'd know what to do when the time came. I know you've always been here for me. And now you're not here. Or are you? You can't tell me what to do, or say. I guess now I have to go on my own. I hope. (*Pause.*) Forgive me mom. It's all I ask. Please. I want you to know. I was afraid I would drown you out with the booze, but I'm happy I didn't. Hell I couldn't. (*Pause.*) Now what? What? (*He starts to hum a song. Frank and Eldon enter carrying torches. Kermit turns and waves to them to join him. Without skipping a beat they join him, holding arms and they sing. Black out. End of Play.*)

JUDY McGUIRE

Interview
(ANGELA SAND)

&

Interview
(DOROTHY)

PHOTO CREDIT: BILL CARLSON FOR ILLUSION THEATER

JUDY MCGUIRE is a writer, director, and multimedia artist living in Minneapolis. She is originally from Roanoke, Virginia, and received a B.A. degree in Anthropology and in English Literature from West Virginia University in 1981. Her work has been produced extensively in the Twin Cities, including productions at Walker Art Center, Red Eye Collaboration, Minnesota Opera, Illusion Theater, and PBS station KTCA. She has been the recipient of two Playwrights' Center Jerome Fellowships, a Minnesota State Arts Board Artist Assistance Grant, a Minnesota State Arts Board Career Opportunity Grant, and is a core member of the Playwrights' Center. She has just been awarded a 1990/91 Bush Fellowship.

I HAVE WRITTEN a series of *Interview* pieces. Each piece is for one performer, and "interviews" a different persona. Included in this anthology are two from the series.

Interview (ANGELA SAND) is first. It was originally written as a Playwrights' Center Jones Commission in January, 1986. The current text is the result of a production at Medium West Image/Text Resource Center in Minneapolis, November 27-December 4, 1987. I would like to credit and thank my collaborators, Carolyn Goelzer and Constance Crawford, for their contributions to the work.

Interview (DOROTHY) is second. It was commissioned and produced for television by PBS station KTCA, St. Paul, and aired February 20 and 24, 1990. Special thanks to Carolyn Goelzer and Barbara Wiener. The current text has been adapted for live performance.

— *Judy McGuire*

(Angela Sand)

The walls on the set are covered with blank, white paper. A homemade time line runs around the bottom of the walls, marked in 100 year intervals. It goes from the present year to "0." Beyond "0," it says "The B.C.," and then a little further on, "The Dawn of Time," with an arrow pointing off the end of the line. This latter part of the line should be placed over a closed door, built into the wall.

Five maps are pinned on the wall. A World map, a map of North America, map of Southeastern U.S., map of Virginia, and a road map of the Eastern U.S.. In another location on the wall there are three diagrams illustrating the use of the Sharp Bond Paper Copier.

In Interview (ANGELA SAND), *the relationship of the performer to the audience is informal.* ANGELA SAND *talks directly to the audience, and charts her thought processes by writing on the paper-covered walls.*

The following page renders what the walls may look like at the end of the piece, not including what is behind the door.

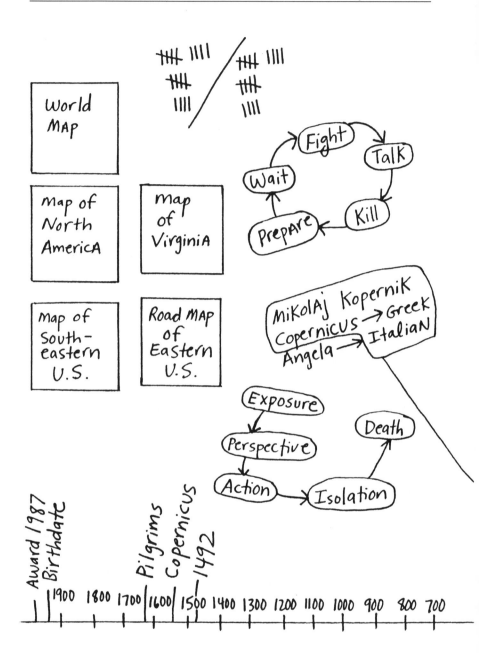

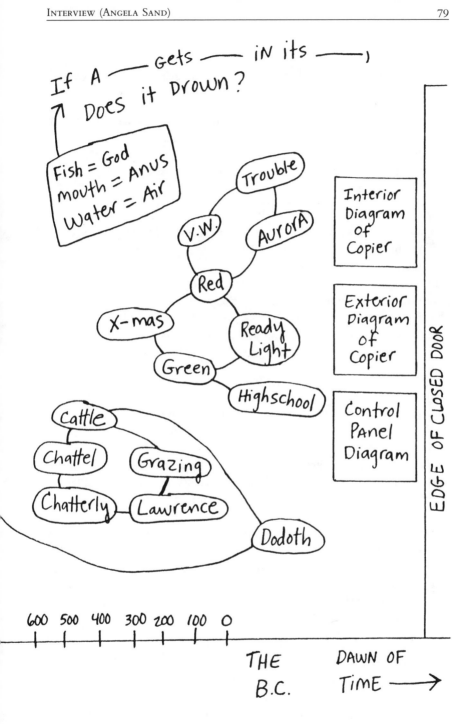

If A ——— gets ——— in its ———,
↱ Does it Drown?

Fish = God
mouth = Anus
Water = Air

Trouble

V.W.

Aurora

Red

X-mas

Ready Light

Green

Highschool

Interior Diagram of Copier

Exterior Diagram of Copier

Control Panel Diagram

EDGE OF CLOSED DOOR

Cattle

Chattel

Grazing

Chatterly

Lawrence

Dodoth

600 500 400 300 200 100 0

THE B.C.

DAWN OF TIME ⟶

You probably don't recognize me away from the Sharp Bond Paper Copier, but you're going to enjoy meeting the woman behind the machine.

I was born and raised in America, in the Southeast, in Virginia, in Culpeper. That's 299 miles from New York City via Routes 29, 211, Interstates 66, 495, 95, and the New Jersey Turnpike. Now I live in Frederick, Maryland. That's 229 miles from the City via Interstates 70, 695, 95, and the New Jersey Turnpike.

I am living approximately 40° latitude north of the equator and 78° longitude west of Greenwich according to my globe. Directly on the other side of the world from me at 40° latitude north and 78° longitude east of Greenwich is the Sinkiang region of China. It is in the western-most part of China, fairly close to the Soviet Union. At first thought, the most awesome thing about the Chinese is that they make up one-quarter of the world's entire population. That's over 1 billion people! But then when you think that now over 55 billion people have been served at McDonald's, the amazing thing is that the Chinese don't eat hamburgers.

A sense of humor separates the men from the boys. This became clear to me when I went home with a friend over Spring Break my sophomore year in college. That was V.C.U., Virginia Commonwealth University, in Richmond, Virginia. Pam, my friend, was from Blackstone, Virginia, and that was about 63 miles from Richmond down Interstate 95 and over on Route 460. I went home with her a few times during college but this was the first time. We were watching "As the World Turns" in the family room, her father was trying to fix the toilet in the downstairs bathroom, and her mother was just starting to fix dinner. Suddenly there's a big crash downstairs. We all run down there and stop at the bathroom door. Pam's father is soaked and a whole half of the toilet bowl is rocking on the blue and gold linoleum floor. For a moment, he looks like he's going to beat it with the wrench, or call it a motherfucker, or ask us what we think we're looking at. But then he says, "Well, I guess there are a lot of half-assed people in this world," and we were all allowed to laugh and I thought, this is brilliant. If I ever meet a man like this I'll marry him on the spot.

Here's the procedure for making copies with the Sharp Bond Paper Copier: First, turn the power switch ON and wait about 30 seconds. The ready light will be a steady red during warm up, and will change to green when the copier is ready. Green is my favorite color. It's lively. It was my high school color. Next, install the paper cassette. Then open the original cover and place the original face down against the guide marks. Close the original cover. You should always keep the original cover closed while making copies. I've been working at the company for six years now. No, make it seven. I tend to leave out the four months I worked over in Finance and the five months in Personnel. My relationship with the company really began when I entered marketing, even though my position as Office Clerk has been pretty much the same in all three departments. But in Marketing, where I have settled, no one has annoying habits and I can pleasantly tap my foot to the rhythm of the Copier and hum along with the I.B.M.. At Christmas this year, Mr. Milton, my immediate superior, gave me a card that said, "Merry Christmas and Best Wishes for the Very Best of New Years." In it, he wrote, "Angela, you're a godsend. You have my vote for Office Clerk of the Year. Thanks a million. Bill Milton." It's nice to know that a person can work hard and be on time and be appreciated. I do do a good job, and keep the office running smoothly. And I was voted Office Clerk of the Year, and received a plaque engraved with, "Angela Sand, Office Clerk of the Year, 1987."

I drive a red 1980 Volkswagen Rabbit. I bought it brand new, and it's been a good car for the 53,841 miles I've put on it, except lately I've been having a little trouble with the carburetor.

The Yupik Eskimo dwell up around 60° latitude north of the equator and 165° longitude west of Greenwich in what is now considered the 49th state in the United States of America. They differ from most Americans in that they do not view the aurora borealis as a breathtaking spectacle, but as an ominous specter of hardship. The worst of all omens is an aurora flashing predominantly red. Such an aurora was noted and feared by the Eskimo for weeks preceding the bombing of Pearl Harbor. But Alaska wasn't a state at the time. And the Eskimo weren't officially Americans. So they didn't consider themselves victims of the red borealis.

We all have some misperceptions about the world. I don't know what yours are, but two of mine have to do with Copernicus. As you know, Copernicus was maligned for being the first to suggest that the earth was not the center of the universe, but orbited around the sun with all the other planets. Copernicus was Greek. Right? Doesn't Copernicus sound Greek to you? Well, he was Polish. His real name was: (writes it out without saying it) Mikolaj Kopernik. Now that's a Polish name. I don't know who decided to dub him Copernicus. The second thing about Copernicus that I was off on was the date of his hypothesis. I didn't exactly place it back in the B.C. with the ideas of Aristotle and Hippocrates, but I did imagine it to be somewhere in the 8th or 9th century A.D.? Wrong. 1543 A.D.. This seemed like a surprisingly late date, but when I remembered that everyone in Europe thought the world was flat up until Christopher Columbus just 51 years before, did I feel dumb. I should have been able to put one and one together, but I have to admit, it slipped right by me.

My parents named me Angela because they are good Christian people. Neither of them is Italian, but my mother's maiden name is Pope.

One of my favorite words is "chattel." It means, property, and the origin of the word is "cattle." I picture Lady Chatterly, grazing on a farm down near Lawrence, Kansas.

A Dodoth tribesman of east Africa is herding cattle at 10° latitude north of the equator and about 33° longitude east of Greenwich. His entire universe is cattle, even down to washing in cow urine and eating the congealed blood as if it were a delicacy. I think these habits are absurd and disgusting, even for a foreigner.

My apartment overlooks the tennis courts. I like to watch people play and even play a little myself. I have one bedroom, a bathroom, kitchen, living room, and a small balcony. I also have lots of closet space. The walls are china white, the woodwork natural, and the carpet a medium blue. I realize that my apartment is basically the same as all the others. I've been in a few. Mine is by far the homiest. I keep the bar stocked and clip out cartoons or articles to hang on the refrigerator. I don't have any pets. I don't have anything against them, but birds squawk, fish are boring, cats scratch up the furniture, hamsters stink, and I saw a dog run over when I was six and can't live with anything I've seen the entrails of.

But I love fresh fish. Especially just breaded and pan-fried. As far as I'm concerned, God could be a fish, somewhere between a rainbow trout and a large-mouth bass. But not a pirate perch. A pirate perch is a small North American freshwater fish that has its anal opening in the throat. I'm sure this is a natural adaptation that suits it very well, but just imagine! And how did it come to be called a "pirate" perch? Does it steal things through its mouth, as fish do, and quick stash them in its anus so no one will want them back? That's ridiculous, I know. Any naturalist around could probably explain it quite logically, but it puts me off. Makes me glad I'm an Aquarius and not a Pisces. I was born on January 29th, 1953. The interesting thing about Aquarius is that while it is symbolized by the water bearer, its element is air. They say this is why your Aquarius lover often seems confused and contradictory, and generally thinks of him-or-herself as enigmatic.

My favorite way to eat an egg is hard-boiled. I know that sounds irrelevant, but just think about it. You always associate solidification with freezing or cooling down, but with an egg it's just the opposite. I like to peel off the shell without having a mess on my hands. And with a little salt and pepper, you can't beat it.

Next, adjust the exposure control. A setting of 1 or 2 is for originals with light pencil or light colored characters. 3 is for ordinary originals. And 4 or 5 is for originals such as newspapers, photographs, and blueprints.

The Pilgrims established a colony at Plymouth in 1620 A.D.. Plymouth is in Massachusetts, and is 221 miles from New York City via Route 44, Interstates 195, 95, and the Connecticut Turnpike. New York City didn't exist in those days, of course, much less the Connecticut Turnpike. Think of how strange it would have been to live back then. Although I suppose living there then wouldn't feel any stranger than living here now. Social scientists say that who you are is completely relative to when and where you were born and what you were exposed to, and I go along with that. I was a Pilgrim in the school play in 3rd grade, and while I was all dressed up like a Pilgrim and hand-dipping candles, I really did feel different.

Mrs. Shockley was my 5th grade teacher. She was incredibly fat but had this wart on the right side of her face that dwarfed all her other features. It wasn't even that big of a wart, but anytime we'd watch a physical fitness film or something where they'd talk about being fat, everyone would start sneaking eyes at her and she'd just turn the right side of her face to us and then all of the sudden all we could see was that wart, and she looked like a tiny speck pinioned behind it.

Spanning around the equator and 38° longitude east of Greenwich is the country of Kenya. Some of the tribes there have a tradition of cutting out all girl children's clitorises before they reach puberty. They say this ensures chastity until marriage and fidelity thereafter. Women of the west are fortunate in that western men already consider them genetically castrated males, and don't feel the need to add injury to insult.

I had sex for the second time when I was seventeen years old and a junior in high school. The first time had been 45 minutes before. The guy was Billy Miller, a senior in my school and my boyfriend at the time. While we were doing it, I looked at his Janis Joplin poster. Iron Butterfly's "In-agadadavida" was on the stereo, and I was thinking about how my younger sister, she was fourteen at the time, said she wanted that played at her funeral. No speeches, no prayers, no nothing, just "Inagadadavida" blasting full out.

My family was on a trip to my aunt's house and stopped at a Truck Stop on Route 211. We usually never stopped on this trip but this time my Dad had a bladder infection and just couldn't make it. And since he was going we all went too, but while everyone else was going I crawled behind the Coke machine. It was warm and tight. And there was some gum stuck on the back. Pink gum, my fingerprint mushed in it, and moist. And a smell that you might not on some days consider a good smell except now it's a feeling, and it hurts to think of not being there smelling it. I saw shoes going by and heard whirring and wanted to die.

If the quality of the copy is unsatisfactory, it's time to change the master. Turn the power switch OFF and open the front cover. Turn the tension lever, open the master cover, and pull the old master out. Next, insert the new master, but use caution. The master is sensitive, be careful not to scratch it. Finally, close the master cover and the front cover and turn the power switch ON. Now you're ready to make a clean copy.

I'm wondering if I should cut my hair. What do you think?

I told you I went to college at V.C.U., Virginia Commonwealth University, in Richmond, Virginia. I wrote a poem my freshman year protesting the Vietnam War. It's called "Counting Poem," and it goes like this:

(*Long pause.*)

Oh, I forgot to tell you that I majored in Business and that Richmond is 335 miles from New York City via Interstates 95, 495, 95, and the New Jersey Turnpike. Let's see. I introduced myself and the Sharp Bond Paper Copier. Told you I was born in Culpeper, but that now I live in Frederick, which is 40° latitude north of the equator and 78° longitude west of Greenwich, and that the Chinese on the other side of the world are not responsible for all those hamburgers. Blackstone. My friend Pam's father. Nice guy, problem with the toilet. Warming up the machine using the ready light to monitor the red and green. Christmas. And my award for being Office Clerk of the Year, which read: "Angela Sand, Office Clerk of the Year, 1987." My car. My carburetor. Customs of the Yupik Eskimo. Red, aurora, Pearl Harbor. Copernicus, which sounds Greek but isn't. Angela which sounds Italian but isn't. And by the way, my mother's name is currently Sand. Words. Chattel, cattle. Dodoth, disgusting. My apartment. My feelings about having pets. My love for fresh fish. The godlike qualities of fish, the not so godlike qualities of the pirate perch. Aquarius, which is my birthsign, January 29, 1953. Exposure control, used to lighten and darken the copies. Mrs. Shockley. Very fat, big wart. Customs in Kenya. Billy Miller, now a postal clerk. Bladder infection. Coke machine. Changing the master. Now these are the Count Up and Count Down keys. Select the number of copies by pressing them. A single copy can be made when the display is zero.

I told you I went to college at V.C.U., Virginia Commonwealth University, in Richmond, Virginia. I wrote a poem my freshman year protesting the Vietnam War. It's called "Counting Poem," and it goes like this:

> Three falling stars and seventy booms,
> Twenty penises
> in fifteen rooms,
> Thirteen thousand
>
> one hundred and sixty-eight bodies
> Found floating face down,
> Twelve metaphors,
> Six feet of ground.

Less than 10° south of the equator and around 140° longitude east of Greenwich live the Dani of New Guinea. They are a dwindling people, with no idea where I live. The various clans are constantly at war with one another and the men make full-time employment out of preparing for the fight, waiting to attack or be attacked, fighting, and then talking about the fight. The warring parties clash in a field, taunting each other and throwing spears back and forth. Everytime a man is killed, his clan is responsible for avenging his death, and having done so, prepares to be a target of revenge. Back and forth it goes on and on, and that's pretty much all the men do with themselves. Except that along with avenging a man's death they have to placate his ghost, and they do this by cutting the first digit off a female relative's finger and burying it in the grave with him. A Dani woman can lose quite a few digits in the course of a lifetime, keeping spirits at bay. And all this has been going on for hundreds of lifetimes, since, who knows when? I was about to say "since the dawn of time," but that is very misleading. True, the Dani have probably lived the same way they are living now for at least a thousand years, but the earth itself is 4½ billion years old, and the universe is estimated at 15 billion. I can give you an idea of the scale.

(*ANGELA opens the door. Behind it, there are colorful dinosaur posters, diagrams and charts representing geologic time to scale, and artists' renditions of the human evolutionary lineage. On the bottom of the inside of the door, there is a continuation of the time line as it is marked on the wall. When the door is fully opened, the line matches up with the one on the wall at "0," and continues backwards, marked with every 100 years B.C. until it disappears into a box mounted on the door.)*

For the first billion years on earth, there wasn't any life. The first life forms were algae and bacteria, growing in the primordial sea. You have to start somewhere. Things literally crept along until about 900 million years ago, when the first oxygen-breathing animals appeared. Then things really got going: First invertebrate forms, first vertebrate forms, first land plants, first amphibians, forests, insects, etc. . .until the Age of Reptiles began about 225 million years ago. That means dinosaurs, and they were the dominant life form on earth for 160 million years. They disappeared suddenly 65 million years ago. The most popular theory is that a huge meteor crashed into the earth and caused a catastrophic change in the earth's environment. Dinosaurs just couldn't adapt. They had become too over-specialized. Plus, they weren't the smartest. A typical stegosaurus had a body 250 times heavier than its brain. So dinosaurs became extinct 65 million years ago, and this gave mammals the chance to flourish. The most rapidly evolving and adaptable mammals were the primates. And from about 15 million years ago, there is fossil evidence of the first humanlike ape, Ramapithecus. From there the clearest line of human evolution seems to be Australopithecus africanus, 4 million years ago, into Homo habilis, 2.5 million years ago, into Homo erectus, 1 million years ago, into Homo sapiens neandertalensis, 150,000 years ago, into Homo sapiens sapiens, 40,000 years ago. Of course, the hard lines are arbitrary, since the process of evolution is imperceptible in a lifetime. But we have been in the same basic form for the last 40,000 years.

(ANGELA removes the box from the door, revealing the time line continuing on, wound on a spindle like an oversized roll of toilet tissue. The end showing reads: "38,012 B.C." ANGELA unrolls it through the following, coming forward in time and letting the paper pile on the floor. Again, the line is to scale, so it is about 400 feet to unroll. She ad libs some commentary during the list as she goes, such as how and why she made the line to scale, and some facts, jokes, and anecdotes about the items listed.)

Through the last Ice Age, Paleolithic toolmakers, cave paintings at Lascaux, Mesolithic and Neolithic toolmakers. First farmers, domestication of animals, City of Jericho, Mesopotamia, Pharaoh Cheops' Great Pyramid and the 100,000 workers working every day for 20 years to build it. Worshippers at Stonehenge, Agamemnon, Trojan War, Olmecs of Mexico, Alexander the Great, the compass.

("The compass" is the first item in A.D., so ANGELA has moved on to the original time line around the wall. Pace accelerates.)

Human sacrifice by the Aztecs, Christian Martyrdom by the Christians, first windmill in Europe, Hildegard von Bingen, Gengis Khan and Kublai Khan, driving the Mongol hordes. Hot-air balloons in China, Columbus, slaughtering of the Incas by the Spanish Conquistadores, Copernicus, Pilgrims, pendulum clock, Betsy Ross, laughing gas, Dostoevski, Darwin. *The Adventures of Huckleberry Finn*, motion picture machine, aspirin, Ford Motor Company, Lillian Gish, World War I, air mail, Matisse. The lost generation, *The Wizard of Oz*, Nazi Germany, nylon stockings, Hiroshima, Ingrid Bergman, Margaret Mead, Mao Tse-tung, frost free refrigerators, my birthdate. Martin Luther King, man on the moon, Chubby Checker, Lady Bird Johnson, Vietnam veterans, "Inagadadavida," pet rocks, punk rock, Momar Khadafy, Bhopal India, Max Headroom, harmonic convergence, and that brings us up to the present moment, where I've been telling you a little bit about myself and the Sharp Bond Paper Copier.

(*Pause.*)

(*ANGELA goes to the copier machine diagrams.*)

When you enter the number of copies and press the Repeat key, the copier will count down as the copies are made until the display reaches zero. To cancel the Repeat function, press the Clear key.

(*She goes to the World map, and pinpoints her exact geographic location. With her finger, she traces a path to a specific spot in the Indian Ocean.*)

On the Globe, the exact adverse of where I live is 40° latitude south of the equator and 78° longitude east of Greenwich. The spot is the belly of the Indian Ocean, but it's not really a place. It's an inconsequential point for saltwater molecules thousands of miles from the nearest continent. No one lives there, but I could go by boat. Transfixed by the heat and largeness of the form, maybe I'd drift right off course and wind up a sparkling fossil in the dunes of the Great Australian Outback.

(Dorothy)

(*DOROTHY stands in front of a large movie screen. The cinematic backdrops are rear-screen projected. She is in her own movie.*)

(*Cinematic backdrop: Technicolor blue sky. Slow moving white clouds.*)

In my neighborhood, there was this story going around that gave me the chills. It was said that if you lit a candle in a dark room, held it under your face and stared at yourself in a mirror while saying, "Mary Worth" 40 times, you would instantly kill yourself. No one knew what it was that happened on the 40th "Mary Worth." No one had ever lived beyond it. But it was said that you saw the face of Mary Worth in the mirror instead of your own, lost your mind, and threw yourself out the window. Now I know that Mary Worth is a comic strip character, but I didn't know that at the time. Whoever made this story up must have had something against the Mary Worth comic strip. But I didn't know there was a Mary Worth comic strip. I was told that Mary Worth was a crazy woman who had committed suicide by throwing herself out a window,

(*Cinematic backdrop: Technicolor blue sky. Faster moving white clouds.*)

so I could see how seeing her face in the mirror in place of your own could cause problems. I had to try it, of course. It wasn't easy to set up. Even though there were candles and matches in both bathrooms for when you took a b.m., it was trouble to be caught playing around with them when you hadn't taken one. My mother had a nose for these things. So I had to try it when she was watching her favorite TV show, and wouldn't budge for an hour. It got dark.

(*Cinematic backdrop: Full moon. Night.*)

My mother finished washing dishes and sat down in front of the TV in the den. I did have my doubts about whether or not Mary Worth had ever existed, but I chose the ground floor bathroom just in case. I closed the door behind me and locked it. This, too, was not allowed. But I could hear the TV. Who would know? The candle was yellow. I lit it first, and then turned off the light.

(*Cinematic backdrop: Technicolor sunset into the ocean.*)

It looked lovely, but that wasn't right, so I thought of terrible things.

(*Cinematic backdrop: A tree engulfed in flames.*)

I pictured myself throwing a boomerang that came back and slammed into my shins. I thought of this anytime I wanted to laugh in an inappropriate place, and it worked well. I wasn't sure it would work for this situation, but it did.

(*Cinematic backdrop: Storm approaching. Late afternoon.*)

I stood in front of the mirror and held the candle under my face. It was eerie. Tense. I started saying, "Mary Worth, Mary Worth, Mary Worth, Mary Worth, Mary Worth," and then realized I could only count on one hand. I would have to divide 40 by 5 and keep track of eight rounds this way. It was too much trouble. I put the candle on the sink to free my other hand — too far from my face. I bent down to the candle — too uncomfortable. The tension dropped.

(*Freeze frame of backdrop*)

I had to get this organized. I looked in the tan plastic trashcan. There wasn't much in it. Mainly Kleenex. I emptied it into the toilet and flushed. I put the trashcan upside down on the sink and placed the candle on it. Pretty good. I stacked a few *Good Housekeeping* magazines under the trashcan. Perfect. I took a couple of big breaths, watching myself in the mirror. I said, "You might throw yourself out the window in a couple of minutes," and it helped put me back in the scene.

(*Release freeze frame.*)

I took a few more big breaths, and started, counting on my fingers: "Mary Worth, Mary Worth, Mary Worth, Mary Worth, Mary Worth, Mary Worth, it was nice having my other hand to count on, Mary Worth, Mary Worth, Mary Worth, Mary Worth, back to the beginning of my first hand, Mary Worth, Mary Worth, Mary Worth, Mary Worth, Mary Worth, other hand, Mary Worth, Mary Worth, Mary Worth, Mary Worth, Mary Worth, back to the beginning of the first hand again, Mary Worth, Mary Worth, Mary Worth, Mary Worth, Mary Worth, other hand, Mary Worth, Mary Worth, Mary Worth, Mary Worth, Mary Worth, back to the beginning of my first hand for the final round, Mary Worth, Mary Worth, Mary Worth. Mary

Worth, Mary Worth, other hand for the last time, Mary Worth, Mary Worth, here goes, Mary Worth, Mary Worth, Mary Worth."

(*Long Pause.*)

(*Cinematic Backdrop: Leader film. No image. Just miscellaneous marks and scratches.*)

I must be doing something wrong. It had to be the counting. I'd been concentrating so hard on counting the "Mary Worths" that I hadn't really been focusing on myself in the mirror. How could your face change into someone else's face in the mirror if you weren't really watching? I would have to do it again. Not counting this time. I figured the 40th "Mary Worth" would come around whether I was counting it or not. And that whatever happened on the 40th "Mary Worth" would happen anyway, catching me by surprise. I could see now that this was how it was supposed to work. I decided to go all out.

(*Cinematic backdrop: View of the Earth from outer space.*)

I would try it in the bathroom on the 2nd floor. I blew out the candle and turned on the light. I put the candle, trashcan, and *Good Housekeepings* back where they belonged. Before going upstairs, I spied in on my mother in the den. She was safely glued to the couch. The upstairs bathroom was pretty much the same as the downstairs bathroom, except for the wallpaper.

(*Cinematic backdrop: Variation of full moon, night.*)

And the candle was red, the plastic trashcan, blue, and the magazines, *National Geographics*. I locked the door and started to set up like before, and then realized I could hold the candle under my face this time since I wasn't going to count the "Mary Worths."

(*Cinematic backdrop: Grand Canyon. Sunset.*)

I couldn't hear the TV up here.

(*Cinematic backdrop: Explosive lava flow.*)

The red candle gave off a more ominous glow than the yellow one had.

(*Cinematic backdrop: Birds startled into flight.*)

Knowing I was next to a 2nd floor window made my stomach flip.

(*Cinematic backdrop: Storm approaching. Late afternoon.*)

This was it. I could see it in my face. I didn't need to say anything to myself. I just stared into my eyes, and started:

(*Cinematic backdrop: Electrical storm. Night. Lightning.*)

"Mary Worth, Mary Worth, Mary Worth, Mary Worth, Mary Worth, Mary Worth, Mary Worth, Mary Worth, Mary Worth, Mary Worth, Mary Worth, Mary Worth, behind me on the wall I could see a large shadow of myself, Mary Worth, Mary Worth, Mary Worth, with an identical, but smaller and darker shadow of myself centered inside it, Mary Worth, Mary Worth, Mary Worth, Mary Worth, Mary Worth, Mary Worth, one shadow must have been caused by me blocking the light from the candle,

(*Cinematic backdrop: Brief dissolve. Endless desert. Day. Then back to electrical storm.*)

Mary Worth, Mary Worth, Mary Worth, and the other by me blocking the light from the reflection of the candle in the mirror, Mary Worth, Mary Worth, Mary Worth, Mary Worth, Mary Worth, Mary Worth, Mary Worth, I wondered which was which, Mary Worth, Mary Worth, Mary Worth, Mary Worth, Mary Worth, Mary Worth, Mary Worth, Mary Worth, the rhythm in my voice made me feel like masturbating,

(*Cinematic backdrop: Brief dissolve. Endless desert. Day. Then back to electrical storm.*)

Mary Worth, Mary Worth, Mary Worth, Mary Worth, Mary Worth, Mary Worth, Mary Worth, I had to be getting close to 40, Mary Worth, Mary Worth, Mary Worth, Mary Worth, Mary Worth, Mary Worth, Mary Worth, Mary Worth, Mary Worth, Mary Worth, Mary Worth, Mary Worth, Mary Worth, Mary Worth, Mary Worth, Mary Worth, Mary Worth, the words were sounding unfamiliar, Mary Worth, Mary Worth, Mary Worth, but I knew that could happen when you said something too many times, Mary Worth, Mary Worth, Mary Worth, Mary Worth, Mary Worth, Mary Worth, Mary Worth, my face was beginning to look unfamiliar, Mary Worth, Mary Worth, but I knew it was still me because of the cat scratch on my forehead, Mary Worth, Mary Worth, Mary Worth, Mary Worth, Mary Worth, Mary Worth, Mary Worth,

(*Cinematic backdrop: Dissolve to endless desert. Day. Wind shifting sand.*)

Mary Worth, Mary Worth, Mary Worth, Mary Worth, Mary Worth, Mary

Worth, Mary Worth."

(*Pause.*)

(*Dorothy smiles.*)

PATRICK SMITH

Driving Around
the House

PATRICK SMITH's other plays include *Embrace the Planet of Emotion, The Secret Gospel of Judas,* and *The Very Last White House Christmas Baby.* His work has been produced around the country by Midwest Playlabs (where *Driving Around the House* was originally workshopped), Brass Tacks Theater, South Coast Repertory Theater, The Asolo State Theater, River Arts Repertory, and Lookout Productions, of which he is a founding member. He holds an MFA from the Tisch School of the Arts, Dramatic Writing Program, and was twice a Playwrights' Center Jerome Fellow during 1985-87.

DRIVING AROUND THE HOUSE is a play that encompasses one year in the life of a five year old boy and his family. It is a series of 40 short scenes, each based on a particular memory, called up by the play's narrator, Grownup Paddy. The scenes unfold onstage in a fluid, continuous motion, punctuated by Grownup Paddy's announcement of the scene titles. These titles function as a kind of instant exposition; Grownup Paddy tells the audience where we are are and what we're doing, so the characters can get right to it.

A common question that has cropped up during production is "how often does Grownup Paddy participate in the action, or interact with his memory family?" Aside from the few moments when the script indicates his active involvement, I would say the other characters ignore him as he observes. His mere presence is the theatrical gesture. This doesn't mean he always sits or stands at the side; he is often smack in the middle of the goings-on, as happy or uncomfortable as the particular memory might make him. The actors and director will naturally discover the moments, and pick the spots, where Grownup Paddy's active involvement, passing an ashtray, or a nudge in the ribs, seems appropriate. Sometimes Grownup Paddy may simply follow his five year old self around.

The play is not conventionally plotted; it is not structured to create suspense. The audience already knows what's going to happen in each scene because Grownup Paddy tells them. The action of each scene is rather commonplace, the ordinary, day to day events of a fairly average childhood. What engages the audience is not *what* happens, but *how* it happens. The play creates Paddy and Grownup Paddy's sense of *wonder* at the extraordinary nature of these ordinary occurences.

My experience is that a simple production works best; a unit set, nothing too fancy. One theatre company mimed most of the props, and that was very successful.

It is the intention of the author that the roles of Paddy and Debbie be played by adult actors.

— *Patrick Smith*

CHARACTERS

GROWNUP PADDY:	Mid to late twenties. Our Guide.
GRAMPA:	Old, crusty.
DADDY:	Early thirties.
MOMMY:	Early thirties.
UNCLE BILLY:	Early forties. A Catholic priest.
PADDY:	Five year old boy
DEBBIE:	Four year old girl.

VARIOUS OFFSTAGE VOICES

SCENE 1: (*Grownup Paddy alone*)

GROWNUP PADDY: Hi, Glad you could make it. We're going on a drive, around and through my house. Sixteen McKinley street. Middletown, Ohio. Nineteen-sixty-three.

I was five.

Here we go.

SCENE 2: (*Grampa, Mommy, Daddy, Paddy, Debbie, in the car.*)

GROWNUP PADDY: A summer's drive down I-Seventy-Five. Grampa's green thunderbird. Nat King Cole sings "Ramblin' Rose" while Daddy drives, left elbow out the window. Grampa rides shotgun wearing a brown felt hat, smoking Camels. Mommy sits in between them with her purse on her lap. Debbie and I are in the backseat; occasionally we stand on the floor and arch our chins over the front seat to talk. As we go past the Seagram's distillery the sweet and acrid smell of cooked alcohol fills the air, a thick odor of burnt soap. I pretend I'm flying above the car like the man on TV who flies along the highway and down into the convertible when the announcer says "Hertz puts you in the driver's seat." Then high concrete walls rise up on either side of us; it's fun to watch the vertical seams rush past the windows. Roger Miller sings "King of the Road" and Grampa lights another cigarette; the smoke gets sucked out the small triangular window in the corner called a *wing*.

SCENE 3: (*Mommy, Daddy*)

GROWNUP PADDY: IN THE BATHROOM.

MOMMY: It's backing into the bathtub again, Pat.

DADDY: Christ. . .I thought that only happened when the toilet flushed.

MOMMY: Well, I told Paddy, but he still flushed it — c'mon in here Paddy! (*Enter Paddy.*) I told him — maybe you should tell him, too.

DADDY: Why'd you flush it when Mommy told you not to? Huh?

PADDY: I know, but I forgot, that's all. I forgot. I'm not an elephant! I forgot and flushed it — I'm not an elephant!

DADDY: Go to bed. (*Exit Paddy, followed by Daddy and Mommy.*)

GROWNUP PADDY: I *am* an elephant.

SCENE 4: (*Grampa, Paddy, Daddy's voice*)

GROWNUP PADDY: IN THE GARAGE.

PADDY: Grampa's playing with me. We're having fun — I think.

GRAMPA: Look at this steam engine, Paddy. It's a toy, but it works the same way as the ones in the powerhouse at Armco. That's where we got those steel ashtrays. Do you know what Armco is?

PADDY: It's where we got those steel ashtrays from.

GRAMPA: Right. It also happens to be where I ruined my health and lost my mind, but those steel ashtrays, right.

PADDY: Why do you have the cord from the coffee pot?

GRAMPA: Don't worry, it'll fit. Now the real powerhouse wasn't electric, we burned coal. Okay, here we go, plug'er in and. . .nothin'. Wait, check the water in the boiler. Plenty of water. Hmmm. Jiggle the cord around.

PADDY: Is it going to work, Grampa?

GRAMPA: Must be a short in this plug. Maybe we could build a little fire underneath it —

DADDY'S VOICE: (*Offstage*) —Dad you do that and you'll burn down the garage!

GRAMPA: Tell you what. You run over to Gillen Crow and pick me up a pack of Camels. Get a dollar from my table, next to my bed. I'll let you spend a nickel. In the meantime, I'll work on this.

PADDY: Okay. (*Paddy exits.*)

GROWNUP PADDY: I was one of the few five year olds who could buy cigarettes in the Gillen Crow Drugstore. The ladies there knew my grandfather sent me. People called him Old Man Smith. We lived in his house on McKinley Street.

GRAMPA: And what the hell's wrong with that?

GROWNUP: Who said anything was wrong?

GRAMPA: Listen, an old man doesn't get dragged into his grandson's story without being accused of *something*. I'm paying attention. I'm keeping track. Don't forget it. (*Paddy enters.*)

PADDY: Watch this, Grampa. Here I go—(*like Superman*)

—up, UP! and A-WAYYYY! (*He flies off.*)

SCENE 5: (*Mommy, Paddy, Debbie*)

GROWNUP PADDY: IN THE BACK YARD.

PADDY: Warm.

DEBBIE: Summer.

MOMMY: Morning.

GROWNUP PADDY: Dazzling sunlight on the clean white sheets Mommy just pulled off the line.

PADDY: Watch this. I can make Mommy sing.

DEBBIE: Make her sing? How?

PADDY: It's a trick. Watch. (*To Mommy*) Red roses, blue lady, red roses, blue lady.

MOMMY: (*Singing*) Send me some
                          red roses
                          for a Blue Lady. . . .

(*To Grownup Paddy*) Oh come on — I didn't go around humming 'Red roses for a Blue Lady' — it had to be something else.

GROWNUP PADDY: (*To Paddy*) Try this instead. Say 'inchworm.'

PADDY: (*To Debbie*) It's a trick, watch. (*To Mommy*) Inchworm.

MOMMY: (*Singing*) Inchworm, inchworm
                          Measuring the marigolds. . . .

Last night I had such funny dreams.

DEBBIE: Did they make you laugh?

MOMMY: I dreamt that we won the Irish Sweepstakes, but we had to go to Ireland to collect it, and we got lost on the way to the airport. But it was still nice. We were all happy, singing in the car — Daddy made me laugh so hard. . . .

PADDY: I dreamed. . .that we had a helicopter!

DEBBIE: Oh you did not.

PADDY: Well, now I am. I'm dreaming of a helicopter. I'm wishing for one.

DEBBIE: That doesn't count. I dreamed we had a pet rabbit. (*To Grownup Paddy*) No! A pet rabbit! That's not good enough! Something better! (*Grownup Paddy whispers in her ear.*) Yes! Last night I dreamed of precious gems and priceless jewels.

MOMMY: When we were little my brother had a camera. I wonder where those pictures are. . . . You know what would be fun, you guys?

PADDY AND DEBBIE: What?

MOMMY: If and when I get my driver's license, I'd drive us out to Hueston Woods on a day like this.

DEBBIE: Without Daddy?

MOMMY: When Daddy has to work. Or when he's. . .busy.

PADDY: A helicopter! Look!

DEBBIE: We could walk to Sunset Pool.

PADDY: I wished for a helicopter and look!

MOMMY: Sunset Pool. Well. It's not a *lake*, like Hueston Woods. No beach, no *sand* to stretch out on. Hot sand and cool, fresh water — when we were in high school that's where Daddy took me on our first date, for a picnic on the beach. We went a lot. On mornings just like this, we'd get up real early; I'd make lunch and he'd drive over. . . .

PADDY: —There it GOES! My helicopter, Mommy!

DEBBIE: Can we go on a picnic?

MOMMY: He never had to work on Saturday before. And it's so pretty out. . . .

PADDY: Daddy goes to work *so much*. He left before I was awake. He got up real early.

GROWNUP PADDY: And then Mommy cried. (*Pause.*)

DEBBIE: Why Mommy?

PADDY: She's not crying. She's not.

MOMMY: That. . .damn inchworm song.

SCENE 6: (*Grampa, Paddy, Debbie*)

GROWNUP PADDY: GRAMPA TELLS PADDY AND DEBBIE ABOUT THE STEEL MILL.

GRAMPA: When I was fourteen, my first job was driving the chairman, Charlie Hook, back and forth between the office and the plant. After I'd been doing that for about six months, one day Mr. Hook leans over the seat and says, "You're a good driver, son. What's your name?" I told him and he says, "Can you repair cars, Billy?" And you know what I told him? I says, "Mister, I can fix *anything* that's busted." What do you think of that?

PADDY: It's funny, Grampa.

GRAMPA: Funny, huh? You've got a strange sense of humor. So Charlie

Hook looks me up and down and says, "How old are you, son?"

DEBBIE: How old are you son?

PADDY: I'm five.

GRAMPA: I said I was seventeen. He looked at me hard and said, "You're a liar. Are you over twelve?"

DEBBIE: Nope. I'm just four. And I can bust *anything*. (*Paddy Debbie laugh like maniacs.*)

GRAMPA: Be nice to your Grampa, now. Then Charlie Hook said, "How'd you like to work in the powerhouse, Billy?" He said I could break in as a mechanic. And I said, "Long as it pays better than driving this car, I'll take it." Then Hook looks at me sideways and says, "You a church goer, Billy?" And I says "Holy Trinity." And you know what he said?

PADDY: Fix my car!

GRAMPA: "Fish-Eater!" He said, "Fish-Eater! You can break in on tindersnapper over to the blast furnace instead."

DEBBIE: Why did he call you that?

GRAMPA: Because he was ignorant. He still did me a favor, getting me a job on the floor. But that tindersnapper was the hottest job in the mill. Still is. Do you know what tindersnapper means? It means a poor dumb-ass who'll catch on fire for money.

SCENE 7: (*Daddy, Mommy*)

GROWNUP PADDY: DADDY RETURNS.

DADDY: I ran into a car. Smacked it good — boom! Hey, let's take the kids out for ice cream, huh?

MOMMY: Are you okay? You're not — was anybody else hurt?

DADDY: Everybody was fine, fine, fine...until they ran me down and punched me.

MOMMY: What?

DADDY: I couldn't get away. C'mon, ice cream or pancakes?

MOMMY: You left the scene of the accident? That's hit and run!

DADDY: It's okay, s'okay, we made a deal, I gave 'em, you know, the insurance thing, the number. . . .

MOMMY: But it expired a long time ago.

DADDY: *They* don't know that. Ha-ha! Dumb bastards. Makes you wonder how people so stupid — beans and cornbread, I bet it causes brain damage. I shoulda said, listen buddy, maybe I put a dent in your car, but you were born with a bigger dent in your head. You got a whole in the head, you dumb briar, and nobody'll ever pay you for it.

MOMMY: You better be more careful. You look. . .sunburned. How's that?

DADDY: Oh I. . .had my lunch hour outside today. It was too nice to stay inside the office all day. How 'bout that ice cream?

MOMMY: Must've been a long lunch hour. Where'd you go?

DADDY: Just sat outside on a bench. Guess we'll skip the pancakes. (*He takes off a shoe. Mommy watches and turns away.*)

MOMMY: Sat on a bench, huh? I s'pose that's how you got sand in your shoes.

SCENE 8: (*Debbie, Mommy, Paddy*)

GROWNUP PADDY: AT THE BREAKFAST TABLE.

PADDY: We're eating bowls of Cheerios—

DEBBIE: —And watching Rocky and Bullwinkle on TV. We've got a dog named Rocky. (*Sound of shrill, irritating barking and howling begins and continues.*) He barks a lot. Last night he knocked me down.

PADDY: Captain Kangaroo comes on next. It's a dark morning.

MOMMY: I'm pouring a cup of coffee for Daddy from the percolator. I like Captain Kangaroo, too. It's a lot smarter than most of the crap on TV. They know a lot of mothers are watching, so they keep the level of things up. (*Enter Daddy.*)

DADDY: This is a dark brown suit I'm wearing for my first day at a new job. That dog is driving me crazy. (*Yells offstage*) Rocky! ROCKY! SHUT THE HELL UP! Christ.

DEBBIE: He likes to bark all right.

DADDY: You saw the dog knock your sister down, Paddy. Why didn't you help her?

PADDY: I couldn't — what if he bit me?

MOMMY: I think that dog is too rough for them. It's hyperactive or something.

DADDY: It's what?

MOMMY: Hyperactive — I read it in Dr. Spock. It means too wound-up all the time.

DADDY: It's just playful, that's all. It's stupid to be afraid of him, he won't bite you.

DEBBIE: He nipped me! It hurt!

DADDY: Cartoons at this hour? Rocky — SHUT THE HELL UP!

PADDY: That's Bullwinkle, Daddy. Rocky's the squirrel.

MOMMY: Nevermind. Here, have some coffee before you run.

DADDY: I'm gonna be late on my first day. That'll impress 'em.

MOMMY: Don't have a wreck, now.

DADDY: Rush hour. In the pouring rain. Yeah.

MOMMY: They won't fire you on your first day, stop worrying.

DADDY: Why won't that dog shut up? Paddy, go see what he wants.

PADDY: But Bullwinkle is on! Make Debbie see.

DEBBIE: Not me! Rocky's too, he's too high-cracked-up, like Mommy said.

MOMMY: I'll see about Rocky, okay? He's just got to bark himself out. He made a mess on the porch — guess who's cleaning *that* up, you guys?

PADDY AND DEBBIE: YUCK!

DADDY: High-cracked-up. That's me. I don't want to go to work today. I don't want to go.

MOMMY: But you've got to — don't you? It's your first day!

DADDY: I'm going. I'm going.

MOMMY: Take your overcoat and umbrella — it's pouring.

DADDY: No. (*He exits.*)

DADDY: (*Offstage*) ROCKY! SHUT THE HELL UP!

SCENE 9: (*Grampa, Mommy and Daddy are playing cards around the dining room table. All three are smoking. Grownup Paddy enters, examining an empty pack of cigarettes. He searches in an ashtray and finds two good-sized butts.*)

GROWNUP PADDY: SMOKE.

Grampa smoked Camels. Mommy and Daddy smoked Kents, except sometimes Daddy smoked a cigar, Dutch Masters. The steel mill smoked bituminous and iron. (*He lights the two butts and sets them in an ashtray. Paddy and Debbie, in pajamas, sneak in. Each takes a smoking butt from the ashtray Grownup Paddy has prepared. They both inhale and cough violently.*)

DADDY: Hey, hey! What're you two doing up?

PADDY AND DEBBIE: (*In between coughs*) We couldn't sleep.

MOMMY: *Like* those cigarette butts? Yuck! I guess you'll never try that again. (*Mommy sings*)

> Mm-mm good
> Mm-mm good
> Cigarette butts are
> Mm-mm good.

GRAMPA: It's those damn Kents, no wonder. I don't know how anybody can smoke those things. Taste just like cardboard. C'mere kids, try one of these.

MOMMY: Dad! They'll think you're serious!

GRAMPA: No sense of humor.

MOMMY: If you two have learned your lesson, you can go back to bed.

DEBBIE: Come up and tell us goodnight.

DADDY: I tucked you in an hour ago.

PADDY: But we woke up again!

MOMMY: Are you having bad dreams? Don't say you're having bad dreams.

DADDY: They're *not* having bad dreams. You're not, are you?

DEBBIE: I dreamed there was a bear in the hall.

DADDY: Not tonight. That was last week, right?

DEBBIE: But it was still scary.

MOMMY: Let's not re-hash our nightmares, tonight, okay Paddy? Don't keep us up all night again.

PADDY: Okay, okay!

DADDY: *Goodnight*, Paddy. *Goodnight*, Debbie. Kiss us goodnight, and back to bed. (*Paddy and Debbie make the rounds for kisses, and exit.*)

MOMMY: (*As Paddy Debbie exit*) Just think about your guardian angels — they're taking care of you. I wonder if Dr. Spock has a chapter on kids' nightmares?

GRAMPA: You don't need that Dr. Spock. Just plain old common sense.

MOMMY: But common sense doesn't apply to dreams.

GRAMPA: You just tell 'em that dreams are all in your head — nothing' to be afraid of.

DADDY: And when Debbie asks *how* they *got in* her head?

MOMMY: And Paddy says he doesn't know how you can tell the difference?

GRAMPA: Well, ask Billy when he gets here. He'll know.

MOMMY: Why should a priest know more than Dr. Spock?

GRAMPA: Bill's studied psychology. He's a man of the world, besides being a priest. *Extremely* bright. He speaks seven languages. He was always Margaret's favorite. (*Enter Uncle Billy, with a metal bar and wall brackets.*)

UNCLE BILLY: This is a chinning bar for the kids. Chinning yourself is excellent exercise. You can hang it in the kitchen doorway. (*To Daddy*) How many pull-ups can you do, mister?

SCENE 10: (*Grampa, Daddy, Uncle Billy*)

GROWNUP PADDY: DADDY WISHES HE COULD TALK TO UNCLE BILLY.

GRAMPA: I picked up a couple cases of beer, Bill. And there's plenty to eat. How long can you stay?

UNCLE BILLY: Long enough to spend some time with you, Dad. The beer's great.

GRAMPA: It's Weidemann. I know you like Weidemann.

UNCLE BILLY: (*To Daddy*) How's your job at . . . the Modern Pawn Shop?

DADDY: Modern *finance* — never a dull moment, you know.

UNCLE BILLY: What's it like, wheeling and dealing in the world of low finance?

DADDY: Sometimes it makes me nauseous.

UNCLE BILLY: You mean *nauseated*. If it makes you *nauseous*, then you're *nauseating* others. Ha!

DADDY: Well, that too, maybe. You look healthy.

GRAMPA: He looks great!

UNCLE BILLY: Isometrics. (*Grampa and Daddy nod, pretending to understand.*) How's your condition, Dad? You look a little skinny.

GRAMPA: I take my insulin injection twice a day; I'm fine.

UNCLE BILLY: Is he fine?

DADDY: Well, he's not getting any worse. We keep an eye on him. You must be tired, Dad.

GRAMPA: Wide awake. But I can take a hint. Goodnight. Nice to have you home, Bill.

UNCLE BILLY: Goodnight, Dad. It's nice to see you again. (*Grampa exits.*) He's okay, huh?

DADDY: Far as anybody knows. Those injections can be trouble. He insists on doing it himself, and he's not too good at it.

UNCLE BILLY: How's everybody else? Healthy?

DADDY: Physically or mentally?

UNCLE BILLY: Either, I guess.

DADDY: Well, everybody's good. Except I'm having a nervous breakdown.

UNCLE BILLY: Uh-huh? Family life gettin' to ya?

DADDY: No, I like it, I do. But I like other stuff, too.

UNCLE BILLY: Such as?

DADDY: I like skipping out of the office after lunch. And just. . .walking around. That's fun in the morning, too. Drink a cup of coffee in a diner, read the paper. Come home and play with my kids. I hate being stuck in that damn office.

UNCLE BILLY: How's that go over with your boss?

DADDY: Not too swift. No, it's a bit risky. But they're so overjoyed to have somebody with an I.Q. over sixty, they're pretending not to notice. I hope.

UNCLE BILLY: So relax. It sounds like an easy-going place. What's the 'other stuff' you like?

DADDY: Well, you know I never would have expected it. I mean, shit, I guess I'm only human, or something, but —

UNCLE BILLY: What the hell are you talking about? (*Enter Paddy.*)

PADDY: Daddy? Daddy, you gotta come up and see Deb.

DADDY: Are you still up? If you've been fighting, you're in big trouble.

PADDY: Debbie's asleep, but she's crying. She's afraid, in her sleep.

DADDY: Oh no. Did you tell her your nightmares again?

PADDY: No! My dream wasn't scary, to *me*. But Debbie—

DADDY: Okay, okay. Go on up, I'm coming. Know anything about kids' nightmares, Bill?

UNCLE BILLY: Not me. But you could look it up in that book by Dr. Spock.

SCENE 11: (*Debbie is fitfully sleeping. Daddy and Paddy beside her bed.*)

GROWNUP PADDY: DEBBIE DREAMS.

DEBBIE: I'm scared. I'm scared. I can't get down.

DADDY: Where are you?

DEBBIE: In the backyard. I'm floating! I'm floating! Help!

DADDY: Grab hold of Paddy's hand.

DEBBIE: I'm floating away!

DADDY: Grab Paddy's hand, he'll hold on to you.

DEBBIE: I can't reach — he's down too far. Help! I'm scared!

DADDY: Paddy can reach you, he can reach you — he's got your hand.

PADDY: Tell her to grab onto the clothesline pole. Don't cry, Deb. It's fun to fly, it's fun.

DEBBIE: I don't like it. I can't get down. I'm floating up. Help!

DADDY: Listen Paddy, I don't think you're helping, so be quiet, okay? (*Enter Mommy.*)

MOMMY: Just wake her up, for God's sake.

DADDY: I did, and she goes right back into it as soon as she falls asleep again.

DEBBIE: I can't get down, it's pulling me up. Daddy!

MOMMY: Did you have to tell her your nightmare? Was it really necessary?

PADDY: I didn't know it was scary — I liked it. Don't be scared, Deb.

DEBBIE: Help me!

DADDY: Listen! Listen to me, Debbie. You're floating down to the ground, now, you're coming down to the back yard, okay?

DEBBIE: Uhh, uhh, uhh. . . .

DADDY: You have to come down now, because — because it's your birthday! You have to come down now because it's time for your birthday party, so you're floating down to the back yard. Are you on the ground now?

DEBBIE: No, I'm still floating!

PADDY: I'm sorry, I'm sorry, I'm sorry. . . .

DADDY: But you're floating back down, okay? You're floating down to unwrap your birthday presents. Think of your birthday — presents and cake with candles and all your cousins at your party. . . .

PADDY: I'm sorry, Mommy.

DEBBIE: My birthday. . .my birthday

DADDY: See all your presents?

DEBBIE: . . . .birthday. . . . .(*snores.*)

MOMMY: (*Whispers*) Nice work, Daddy. Let's all go to sleep, goodnight, Paddy. You think of your birthday, too. Good night, sleep tight, I love you and I like you, you're the best boy in the world, and what's tomorrow?

PADDY: Tuesday?

MOMMY: Good guess. Thursday. (*Mommy and Daddy exit.*)

PADDY: I didn't mean to scare you, Deb. I'm sorry. (*Paddy sleeps. Grownup Paddy picks him and carries him, flying, around the room.*)

SCENE 12: (*Living room tableau. Illustration of Grownup Paddy's monologue. Paddy and Debbie sneak up and spy on the scene.*)

GROWNUP PADDY: CHRISTMAS EVE. A shiny aluminum tree changes colors in the light of a lamp with revolving red, blue, yellow and green filters. Daddy is on the floor, sipping a beer, happily engrossed in arranging an elaborate battle landscape with army men, trucks, jeeps and artillery. Uncle Billy is vigorously exercising with various body-building devices, while reciting the liturgy of the Mass in Latin. Mommy is singing "Ramblin' Rose," surrounded by heaps of wrapping paper and ribbon. She is tagging presents. Grampa is dozing in an armchair. He wakes, lights a Camel, changes the channel on the TV, does not turn up the volume. He gets up and shifts the revolving lamp around the living room to find the perfect position.

GRAMPA: Turn on the radio. Midnight Mass from St. John's is on WPFB.

UNCLE BILLY: It's one-thirty, Dad. You missed it.

GRAMPA: What the hell are we all doin' up so late?

UNCLE BILLY: This is how your grandson remembers it. He thinks it's funny. (*A telephone rings. Paddy and Debbie jump out of sight.*)

MOMMY: Who'd be calling at this hour?

UNCLE BILLY: Maybe it's Uncle Chester calling from jail. The man really gets the Christmas spirit. Remember the Christmas Eve, Dad, when Uncle Ches' called to get bailed out of the tank? (*Exit Uncle Billy.*)

GRAMPA: Ches' has been on the wagon fifteen years. Diabetes. He had a sense of occasion all right. He was tickled to death when your mother answered the phone. "Merry Christmas, Margaret," he says, "This is your brother Chester, calling from jail." Your mother dropped her rosary into her beer. (*Enter Uncle Billy.*)

UNCLE BILLY: It's for you, Pat.

DADDY: Oh yeah? Huh. ...

MOMMY: Who's calling? (*Exit Daddy. He reappears in a dim hallway with telephone. Paddy and Debbie sneak up and spy on him.*)

UNCLE BILLY: Somebody Clark. Works at Modern Finance with him. He's had a dose of holiday cheer, I'll tell you that.

DADDY: Hello?

WOMAN'S VOICE ON PHONE: Merry Christmas, baby.

DADDY: Oh! Hi! Merry Christmas to you, too, Clark! Why're you calling so late, ol' buddy?

WOMAN'S VOICE ON PHONE: I made Clark call, in case you didn't answer. Smart, huh?

DADDY: Brilliant. But this isn't a good time to talk business, Clark. Merry Christmas, how're you doing?

WOMAN'S VOICE ON PHONE: Lousy. We're having a little party. You should be here. Rose and Clark are here. They're having fun. But I don't have a partner, baby.

DADDY: Where's Roy?

WOMAN'S VOICE ON PHONE: He's on the the first leg of a double at the open hearth. I'm mad at him. Can't you come over, baby?

DADDY: I've got to say good-bye now. You have a merry Christmas, uh...Clark.

WOMAN'S VOICE ON PHONE: Tell me you love me, baby.

DADDY: Count on it.

WOMAN'S VOICE ON PHONE: Tell me baby. I'm lonesome.

DADDY: First thing at work on Monday morning. I'll give you all the details. Merry Christmas. Good night.

WOMAN'S VOICE ON PHONE: Tell me you love me. Whisper it. Nobody'll hear you.

DADDY: (*Whispering*) Good night, Clark. I love you.

(*Paddy and Debbie look at each other.*)

SCENE 13: (*Daddy and Paddy on the floor.*)

GROWNUP PADDY: THE SHOE TYING LESSON.

DADDY: Watch what I do. First over and under. Then a loop, and around, and another loop through the middle. See? I'll do it again, real slow. Over and under, loop, around, another loop through the middle. Okay? Now you try it.

PADDY: Okay. Umm. . . .

DADDY: Over and under —

PADDY: — oh yeah. Then like this and —

DADDY: — no, around first, then —

PADDY: — a loop and it goes through —

DADDY: — no, look. You've got it backwards. *Watch* this time. See. Try it again.

PADDY: First this, then, um, around here, and, then what?

DADDY: Think. What does a bow look like?

PADDY: Well. . . .

DADDY: It's got two loops, right? A bow has two loops, so what do you need to make?

PADDY: Ahh. . .I don't know.

DADDY: Think!

PADDY: Um, like this?

DADDY: No! You need another loop! I'll show you again. Now will you just look? It's easy. You surprise me, Paddy. You're old enough to learn this. Are you watching? Huh?

PADDY: Yes!

DADDY: Around and under, a loop, around and another loop through the middle. Got it?

PADDY: I think so.

DADDY: Go ahead, then.

PADDY: First around here, then, like this—

DADDY: — right, good.

PADDY: And through here and. . . .

DADDY: . . .yeah, then?

PADDY: Then here?

DADDY: No! Think, Paddy! You're not thinking! Wake up!

PADDY: I'm trying! I'm thinking!

DADDY: Start over. I know you're smarter than this, Paddy. You've got to watch and think!

PADDY: Okay! Um, around and then under —

DADDY: — no! Were you watching me or not! Were you watching me?

PADDY: Yes! Can I try again later, Daddy?

DADDY: No, we're going to get this right. It's easy. Just tie your shoe and I'll let you go. Go ahead, do it.

PADDY: This, then here, then around and another loop. . . .

DADDY: Almost, then the last thing. Are you thinking?

PADDY: Uh-huh, like, uh, this?

DADDY: No! Why can't you get it? Are you sleepy?

PADDY: No, I just...can I try again later on, Daddy?

DADDY: We're going to get this right, *now* not later. (*Enter Mommy.*)

MOMMY: I think that's enough for the first lesson. Let him go.

DADDY: He's smart enough to do this. He can learn it right now. Start over. *Think* this time. (*Paddy's hands are shaking.*) What's the matter. You really surprise me, Paddy. I thought you were pretty smart.

MOMMY: Let him go — he'll get it the next time.

DADDY: Mary Ann.

MOMMY: Let him go.

DADDY: He's got to learn to think.

PADDY: I'll get it next time, Daddy. I promise.

MOMMY: Daddy knows you will. You can go outside now. (*Exit Paddy.*)

DADDY: He could've gotten it right. I know it. Where's Debbie? Let's see if she —

MOMMY: — She's taking a nap! Besides she's only four years old.

SCENE 14: (*Daddy, Mommy, Grampa, Uncle Billy playing poker. Piles of poker chips.*)

GROWNUP PADDY: WE CHASE THE SPOTLIGHT.

DADDY: What's that?

UNCLE BILLY: What?

GROWNUP PADDY: Daddy ran to the window.

DADDY: There's a light in the sky — some kind of spotlight.

UNCLE BILLY: I wonder what it is?

GRAMPA: C'mon, dammit. Finish the hand.

MOMMY: I'll call. What've you got?

DADDY: It's bright, isn't it?

GRAMPA: Pair of jacks, ace high.

UNCLE BILLY: Could be a movie premier.

DADDY: In Middletown?

MOMMY: Full house.

GRAMPA: Christ.

UNCLE BILLY: Wanna go see what it is?

DADDY: We'll bring the kids. C'mon.

MOMMY: But they're in their pajamas!

UNCLE BILLY: It's not cold outside.

DADDY: Paddy! Debbie! C'mon in here — we're going for a ride.

MOMMY: You guys are crazy.

GRAMPA: Yep. (*Enter Paddy and Debbie.*)

PADDY AND DEBBIE: What? What're we doing?

MOMMY: Daddy and your uncle are taking you out to catch pneumonia.

DEBBIE: Huh?

DADDY: Take a look out the window — see that light?

UNCLE BILLY: We're going to find out what it is.

DADDY: I love stuff like this.

GRAMPA: Anything out of the ordinary and they go into ecstatic fits.

UNCLE BILLY: Get in the car, whoever's going. You got the keys?

DADDY: We'll be back in awhile.

MOMMY: I hope they're not too drunk. (*Exit Daddy, Uncle Billy, Paddy, Debbie.*) Grab a blanket for the kids! (*Scene shifts to the car.*)

GROWNUP PADDY: We got in the car, in our pajamas with a blanket in the back seat. Daddy drove while Uncle Billy navigated.

UNCLE BILLY: The gas tank is empty!

DADDY: No it's not — I know there's a little left. Which way should I go?

PADDY: There it goes!

DEBBIE: What's it a light for?

PADDY: Somethin' *fun*, huh, Daddy.

UNCLE BILLY: I'd try out by the shopping center.

DEBBIE: Can we go in a store in our pajamas? I'm wearing the blanket!

DADDY: I'm gonna head down Central.

DEBBIE: There it goes again! It goes up to the clouds!

DADDY: What's the speed of light, Paddy?

PADDY: Ask Debbie — I don't know.

UNCLE BILLY: I don't think his first grade class has tackled quantum physics yet. There it goes — take a left, take a left!

DADDY: They might be giving away free samples, you guys.

PADDY: Free samples of what?

DADDY: Is light a wave or a particle?

DEBBIE: I wave at the moon sometimes. Hi, Mr. Moon!

PADDY: It's getting brighter!

UNCLE BILLY: Turn right here. Here!

DADDY: Okay. Shit, it's a one way street! Is anybody coming?

UNCLE BILLY: Go ahead. You know what? I think it's at Wilson's Funeral Home.

DADDY: Forget about free samples. We don't want any.

UNCLE BILLY: We're on top of it — next left!

DADDY: It's not the funeral home — it's behind it. The light's bigger than I thought. What could it be, you guys?

DEBBIE: Free ice cream!

PADDY: The June Taylor Dancers!

GROWNUP PADDY: Through the nighttime streets our intrepid T-bird sped, in search of the source of the mysterious spotlight, until finally we found it — there on the corner of Grand and Main.

DADDY: There it is! Look kids, it's a, it's a, it's the grand opening of. . . what?

PADDY, DEBBIE, UNCLE BILLY: A new gas station!!!

DADDY: Lucky thing — we're empty.

SCENE 15: (*Daddy sits alone at a table full of beer bottles.*)

GROWNUP PADDY: DADDY'S MISTRESSES. The go-go dancer. The rich heiress. The college co-ed. The former nun. The charming divorcée. The professional golfer. The nuclear physicist. The fading starlet. The fugitive murderess. The KGB spy. (*Daddy slumps to the floor and crawls away on hands and knees.*)

SCENE 16: (*Uncle Billy is on the phone. Mommy, Daddy and Grampa are eavesdropping. Paddy and Debbie are spying on Mommy, Daddy and Grampa.*)

GROWNUP PADDY: UNCLE BILLY'S PHONE CALL.

UNCLE BILLY: Merde!

GRAMPA: What's he saying?

DADDY: It's French, Dad. I think it means —

MOMMY: — shhh! He's talking to *her.*

GRAMPA: *Her* who?

UNCLE BILLY: Mais qu'est-ce que tu veux?

GRAMPA: Who the hell is he talking to?

MOMMY: Nobody. Somebody he met in France.

UNCLE BILLY: Mais je t'adore, tu le sais.

DADDY: He left a French-English dictionary around here, somewhere. (*Daddy looks for it.*)

UNCLE BILLY: T'es fou!

GRAMPA: Wait a minute, he's calling *France* on *my* phone? He could've asked me first.

MOMMY: It might be a local call, you don't know.

GRAMPA: Who the hell speaks French in Middletown?

DADDY: Here's the dictionary.

UNCLE BILLY: Je m'en fou! Tu compris?

DADDY: Foo. Oh I know. It means crazy.

GRAMPA: I'm not surprised.

MOMMY: Maybe they're planning a secret rendez-vous.

UNCLE BILLY: Je ne sais pas, hein? Je ne sais pas! Mais bien sur, je t'aime! Merde!

DADDY: I think he's arguing about sex.

GRAMPA: Now who'd argue with a priest about sex? C'mon.

UNCLE BILLY: D'accord, d'accord! Ca suffit, hein? A bientôt, je promis. Je t'embrasse, je t'aime. Oui. Alors. 'Bye. (*He hangs up. All pretend to be preoccupied. Uncle Billy enters the living room.*)

MOMMY: We're pretending to be preoccupied.

UNCLE BILLY: Eavesdropping, eh?

GRAMPA: You *know* we were. Why else were you speaking French? What the hell's going on here?

UNCLE BILLY: I'm leaving the priesthood. I'm going to marry a Jewish violinist from Paris, and live in New York City. Satisfied? (*Grampa bursts out laughing.*)

GRAMPA: Haww! No, really. What's going on?

UNCLE BILLY: That's it. I'm not pulling your leg. I'm getting married.

MOMMY: I'm so happy for you, Bill. Congratulations.

GRAMPA: What'd you do, get some girl pregnant? You don't have to marry her, don't be stupid. Happens all the time. You think Thomas Merton didn't fool around? Saint Francis, even.

UNCLE BILLY: I need a beer.

DADDY: Me too. (*He exits.*)

UNCLE BILLY: Her name is Nadja, Dad. And she's not pregnant. I'm marrying her because I love her. More than anybody I've ever known.

GRAMPA: Your mother is turning over in her grave. Like a rotisserie. (*Enter Daddy with beer.*)

DADDY: Here you go, Bill. Congratulations.

SCENE 17: (*Uncle Billy, Mommy*)

GROWNUP PADDY: TAKING DOWN THE CHRISTMAS TREE.

UNCLE BILLY: Did my brother make the *creche*?

MOMMY: The nativity scene? Yes. Tim made it. It's pretty, isn't it? I think he's really talented.

UNCLE BILLY: It's a bit more realistic than that cement madonna in the back yard.

MOMMY: But I like that, too. It's kinda different.

UNCLE BILLY: How did we start talking about it?

MOMMY: Talking about what?

UNCLE BILLY: About whether or not we *like life*.

MOMMY: I was surprised when you said you didn't.

UNCLE BILLY: Well, I don't.

MOMMY: But how can you say that?

UNCLE BILLY: I appreciate the importance of the journey...but I do not *like* it.

MOMMY: Uh-huh. That's what you said.

UNCLE BILLY: It has a ring to it, doesn't it? I appreciate the importance of the journey, but I do not *relish* it. That's better. I do not *relish* it.

MOMMY: I think it sounds grim. Or I don't get it. (*Pause.*) Well, take Thomas Merton.

UNCLE BILLY: Yeah?

MOMMY: You were in the Trappist monastery, where he was.

UNCLE BILLY: Gethsemene.

MOMMY: Does *he* like living?

UNCLE BILLY: I doubt he'd acknowledge the question.

MOMMY: (*Pause.*) Look, do you like Nat King Cole?

UNCLE BILLY: Well, yeah. I like his records a lot.

MOMMY: Then you like life. You do.

SCENE 18: (*Daddy and Uncle Billy are drinking beers. Paddy and Debbie wear beer cartons on their heads. Grownup Paddy drinks a beer and watches.*)

GROWNUP PADDY: UP AT THE LIVING ROOM CEILING.

UNCLE BILLY: Here you go! (*He lifts Debbie up and holds her horizontally above his head.*)

DEBBIE: Uncle Billy, I don't think I like it up here very much —

UNCLE BILLY: — Look at the ceiling! Ever seen it that close up before?

DEBBIE: No. Okay, down now, please. (*Daddy lifts Paddy in the same way.*)

PADDY: HaHa, I'm not afraid! Hi Debbie. Are you afraid?

DEBBIE: No, uh, no, not me.

DADDY AND UNCLE BILLY: Here we GOOOOOOOOOOOOOOOO! (*The two men rush around the room, holding the terrified babies aloft.*) WAAAAA-HOOOOOOO! (*Enter Mommy.*)

MOMMY: Hey you guys — put them down. You're scaring them to death. (*Enter Grampa.*)

GRAMPA: What the hell's goin' on down here? I was tryin' to take a nap.

UNCLE BILLY: Sorry Dad. Just having a little fun with the kids.

GRAMPA: Some damn fine example you set. My sons. Unrepentant drunks. (*To Mommy*) What made you marry the likes of him?

MOMMY: Hey — don't rub it in.

UNCLE BILLY: Let me tell you a story about your Grandpa, Paddy and Debbie. One day your Grandpa and his pals were driving around in this old Packard, going from bar to bar. It must've been payday at the mill. Wahoo! Well, Dad's at the wheel and BAM! He slams the car into something. What was it? He rear ended a parked cement mixer! Broke his nose, knocked a quarter panel off the Packard, and made the machine dump about a half ton of cement. But nothin' serious. The boys got out, wired the car back together, wiped the cement off the windows, and drove on to the next bar. They got caught, though. It wasn't too tough — the police just had to look for a car with wet cement all over it. And the guy with the nose on the other side of his face, he gave it all away. (*Pause, Grampa looks stern. Then smiles.*)

GRAMPA: You wanna know somethin' funnier than that story, Bill? *You* marrying a Jewish violinist from France.

SCENE 19: (*Grampa, Paddy*)

GROWNUP PADDY: GRAMPA EXPLAINS ABOUT CATHOLICS IN MIDDLETOWN.

GRAMPA: Go ahead, ask me something.

PADDY: Why don't you go to mass at St. John's, like me and Debbie and Mommy and Daddy?

GRAMPA: Because I belong to the Holy Trinity parish.

PADDY: Oh yeah.

GRAMPA: That's the church with the stained glass window of your patron saint. You've been there with me lots of times.

PADDY: I know.

GROWNUP PADDY: There were many Sundays when I went to mass twice. First to St. John's with my parents and my sister, then to Holy Trinity with my grandfather. (*Enter Mommy.*)

MOMMY: Today he was *chewing* the back of the pew. A boy his age! You don't let him do that in Holy Trinity, do you?

GRAMPA: Mary Ann, I have never seen him chew on a pew. Ever.

MOMMY: You think it's funny! He was digging his teeth into the scrollwork. He's too big to behave that way. Aren't you?

PADDY: Yes!

GROWNUP PADDY: But it felt really good to sink my teeth into the sacred woodwork.

GRAMPA: Your mother, Paddy, is a member of the St. John's parish. It's the German parish.

MOMMY: And Polish. And Italian. And Slovak. And there are Irish families, too, some.

GRAMPA: Not real ones. And they don't have a stained glass window of St. Patrick, do they, Paddy?

MOMMY: We have plenty of saints, too. And I think the altarpiece at St. John's is much prettier. I'm not going to argue. Your father loves to argue, too, Paddy. I can't imagine where he gets it from. (*Exit Mommy.*)

GRAMPA: There's St. Peter Claver, where the colored people go. And St. Mary's where the east end rich people go.

PADDY: Is everybody in Middletown Catholic?

GRAMPA: No. There are Presbyterians, Episcopalians, Methodists, Lutherans, Baptists, Seventh Day Adventists, Holy Rollers. The Holy Rollers roll around the floor in their churches. And Pentecostalists play with big poisonous snakes. But the thing is, they're all Protestant.

PADDY: What does that mean?

GRAMPA: It means they're all going to hell when they die. They're in for a shock. I'd love to see the look on their faces.

PADDY: Catholics don't go to hell, do they?

GRAMPA: Well, some do. There are bad ones. But they get excommunicated. That means they get kicked out.

PADDY: What for?

GRAMPA: Big sins. People who get divorced, you know, they leave their husbands or wives. Unless you're rich. Then you can divorce you r wife and write a letter to the Pope. And he'll let you stay in. But don't you worry about that. Just remember the Holy Trinity parish is the Irish parish, the best and the truest Catholic.

MOMMY: (*Offstage*) Then why is the Pope Italian?

GRAMPA: But he wishes he was Irish.

SCENE 20: (*The kitchen. Paddy, Debbie, Mommy, Daddy*)

GROWNUP PADDY: DADDY MAKES AN ABACUS.

DADDY: We need a cigar box, some coat hangers and the red wire cutters. Where are the red wire cutters? How's the Play-Doh doing? (*Mommy looks into the oven.*)

MOMMY: Uh-oh, Pat. The little rings are crumbling.

PADDY: Oh no! Why are they crumbling?

DADDY: It seemed like a good idea. Oh well.

MOMMY: Well, whoever heard of telling kids to make a, what's it called?

PADDY: An abacus, Mommy! How many times do I have to tell you? An abacus! An abacus! An abacus!

DADDY: Calm down before I say the hell with your abacus, boy.

DEBBIE: Why is Paddy crying?

MOMMY: If he doesn't bring an abacus in this morning, he's afraid he'll be drummed out of kindergarten.

PADDY: Everybody else will have one! I'll be the only one without an abacus.

MOMMY: What I want to know is —

DEBBIE: — Mommy what's an ackabus?

MOMMY: — why did you wait until Monday morning before school to start this little project? And why, why, why an abacus? What happened to the new math? It's the goddam space age and they tell him to build an abacus. A home-made abacus. I bet people with money just go out and *buy* a lousy abacus for their kid, and skip the educational bullshit. Sorry, I got carried away. Oh my.

DEBBIE: Daddy what's an ackabus?

DADDY: The space age. The rocket! I forgot! (*Daddy turns on the TV.*) The Mercury Rocket, you guys! It's counting down!

PADDY: Daddy I need an abacus, not a rocket.

DEBBIE: WHAT IS AN ACKABUS?

MOMMY AND DADDY: No shouting!

PADDY: Dear God please help me to make this abacus, please God please.

DADDY: Oh stop that, you can't pray for an *abacus*.

MOMMY: Well he can pray for help. That's okay.

DEBBIE: He needs it.

PADDY: Shut up dumbo!

MOMMY: Don't call your sister dumbo.

DADDY: T-minus two minutes and counting. An abacus is a counting advice that dates from ancient times. A frame containing parallel rods with beads that slide up and down. This cigar box is our frame. Using the red wire cutters, I snip parallel rods from several wire coat hangers to fit the box.

PADDY: But the Play-Doh didn't work. We don't have any beads. Dear God please help us to figure out something, please, God, please.

DADDY: Yes. I admit the failure of my Play-Doh plan is a set back, but only a temporary one. T minus one minute and —

MOMMY: Remember this, you two: Never have children before you're rich.

DADDY: Beads, beads, beads. Why didn't the Play-Doh work? Stuff drys hard as a rock if you don't want it to.

PADDY: We have to catch the bus in twenty minutes! C'mon God, twenty minutes!

DEBBIE: I hope I never have to make an abacus. Christ Almighty. I believe I will have some more Cheerios. (*She pours herself some.*) Milk please! Milk please!

MOMMY: What's that smell? Something burning in the oven? My God it's the Play-Doh. It's on fire! (*Mommy pulls a tray of flaming Play-Doh crumbles from the oven.*)

DEBBIE: Will someone pour some milk on my Cheerios? The carton is too heavy for me.

DADDY: What a stench! T minus ten, nine, eight, seven —

DEBBIE: Milk please.

MOMMY: (*Choking and sneezing from the smoke.*) I think those fumes are lethal. Tuberculosis is setting in.

DADDY: Three, two, one, zero, ignition, lift-off! Yeah! Look at it go! That's an atlas booster, the astronaut is in the capsule at the top. He eats his food from tubes, like toothpaste. Do you think it's going to blow up? You should say a prayer for the astronaut.

DEBBIE: How do they get Cheerios into a tube?

DADDY: Cheerios! That's what we'll use for the abacus! Cheerios!

MOMMY: Smart!

PADDY: Thank you, God. Now please make sure we catch the bus.

DADDY: Don't I get any credit?

DEBBIE: I NEED MILK ON MY CEREAL!

DADDY AND MOMMY: No shouting!

SCENE 21: (*Mommy, Paddy*)

GROWNUP PADDY: MOMMY GREETS PADDY AFTER A DAY AT SCHOOL.

MOMMY: And what did you do at school today?

PADDY: We had to tell what church we go to.

MOMMY: Uh-huh. What did you tell your teacher?

PADDY: I said we go to two churches, St. John's and Holy Trinity.

MOMMY: (*Laughing*) Oh. But you could've just said St. John the Baptist. If she asks again, you can say St. John's. That's easier.

PADDY: But we go to both!

MOMMY: I know, but your teacher might think that's a little weird, that's all. Do you know *why* she asked what church we attend?

PADDY: She asked everybody.

MOMMY: Yes but why. Do you know?

PADDY: She had to write it on a card.

MOMMY: Okay. What else did you do today? Did you learn anything new?

PADDY: I asked Mrs. Layton why the moon follows our car along the road.

MOMMY: And what did she say? Did she explain why it *looks* that way, but it's really not moving?

PADDY: She said she didn't know. I told her it's because the moon likes us.

SCENE 22: (*Daddy, Mommy, Paddy, Debbie*)

GROWNUP PADDY: THE BACK SEAT OF THE '57 CHEVY. The black and white Chevrolet classic. Grey and black upholstery. Daddy's pride. *His* car, not Grampa's. Debbie and I sit in the back, balancing huge hot fudge sundaes from the Dairy Queen in our laps. We're cruising Middletown's expensive east end. Daddy and Mommy are admiring the splendid estates, while the sundaes are melting, the vanilla and fudge dripping in ever-increasing rivulets into our laps, onto our bare legs and over the back seat. "Puff the Magic Dragon" plays on the radio. Later tonight Daddy will leave the keys in the car, and it will be stolen from the curb in front of our house. Lost. But for now, Daddy puts his arm around Mommy, and turns around to smile at us. He says:

DADDY: My God! The upholstery!

GROWNUP PADDY: Mommy and Daddy frantically mop with tiny napkins that disintegrate into fuzz. The back seat and our suntanned knees are covered with fudge syrup and little bits of white fuzzy paper.

SCENE 23: (*Daddy, Mommy*)

GROWNUP PADDY: DADDY CONFESSES.

DADDY: I hurt somebody.

MOMMY: Oh yeah? Somebody besides me?

DADDY: I knew I . . . I knew it could only turn out bad, and I did it anyway.

MOMMY: Um, I'm not sure if I really want to hear your confession.

DADDY: I did it anyway. I knew it and I did it anyway. I wanted it.

MOMMY: Say three Hail Marys and go to bed. In the morning you won't remember a thing.

DADDY: But you wanna know the funny thing?

MOMMY: No.

DADDY: The funny thing was. . . .

MOMMY: . . . will you please go to bed and leave me alone?

DADDY: The funny thing was that I was thinking about you the whole time.

MOMMY: That's hysterical.

DADDY: I was worried about hurting *you*. Not her. Stupid. I'm stupid.

MOMMY: You're drunk. And I'm tired. Don't talk to me anymore.

SCENE 24: (*Grampa and Paddy sit together. Grampa smokes.*)

GROWNUP PADDY: ON THE FRONT PORCH GLIDER. I don't know if they still make them, but a *glider*, or the kind we used to have on the front porch, is a piece of patio furniture, like a couch that you could rock back and forth in. Not like a rocking chair, because a glider doesn't tilt back, it's got a track with springs between the seat and the legs that allows the seat to slide forward a few inches and back a few inches. They're usually covered with big floral pastels in canvas or oilcloth. The glider on our front porch squeaked when you rocked it—

GRAMPA: — only because I got sick and tired of being the only one who would take the trouble to *oil* it.

PADDY: But I like the squeaky noise, Grampa.

GROWNUP PADDY: Me too.

GRAMPA: Let me tell you something about women. Your grandmother died before you were born, but she was a woman. She thought she was an angel or a goddess. So did I. Walk by her room at four o'clock in the morning and she'd be there kneeling beside her bed, praying. She lived a large part of her life in her own imagination. Got so she was afraid to go out of the house. Agoraphobia, they call it, now. I did all the shopping. Even her clothes. I'd pick out a selection of dresses and bring 'em all home for her to choose from. What do you think of that?

PADDY: I don't know, Grampa.

GRAMPA: Me neither. Anyway, women. I'll tell you right now, they're going to drive you crazy, so don't be surprised when it happens. One of these days you're going to get married. Before you're married they call it 'sowing your wild oats' but after you're married it's adultery. Do you understand what I'm telling you?

PADDY: No grampa.

GRAMPA: Good. The main thing about women is this: the girls you get *excited* about are *bad* for you, the ones you *marry*, they're even — wait a minute, there's a damn bumblebee— (*Grampa whips off his shoe and swats it against the floor viciously.*) —got him, dammit! So never forget that, Paddy, all right?

SCENE 25: (*Paddy, Grampa, Daddy*)

GROWNUP PADDY: A GOOD NIGHT KISS, the taste of beer on my father's lips. His brown wing tips in the bottom dresser drawer. His shoe shine brushes, the cans of kiwi polish, the smell like the waxy banisters in St. John's stairwell, cool and dark. His imitation tortoise shell cigar holder. His laugh, a high, short burst. Staccato and frequent.

SCENE 26: (*The living room. Paddy and Debbie watching TV. Enter Daddy.*)

GROWNUP PADDY: DADDY TELLS PADDY AND DEBBIE THAT SANTA CLAUS IS A FAKE.

DADDY: How can you guys watch Uncle Al every single day?

PADDY: I don't know. I like it.

DEBBIE: Sometimes they have fun things, animals and puppets. (*Daddy turns off the TV.*)

DADDY: You should make your own puppets. No more uncle Al. That's it.

PADDY: But I like it!

DEBBIE: We can't watch Uncle Al ever again? Ever?

DADDY: You're too old for Uncle Al.

PADDY: But the kids on the show are the same as us! They're five, too.

DEBBIE: I'm four, I'm not too old.

DADDY: Listen, Uncle Al is a *fake*. Nobody wears a straw hat, a plaid jacket and carries an accordion around all the time. He's just a fake, understand?

PADDY: But he's on TV.

DADDY: Stuff on TV isn't *real*, it's just made-up. You know that, don't you? Or haven't I taught you anything?

DEBBIE: President Kennedy was on last night. You made us watch *that*.

PADDY: But that's the news, dumbo.

DEBBIE: Oh.

DADDY: There's a difference between the news and Uncle Al.

DEBBIE: But sometimes Uncle Al is *on* the news — he says the sports.

DADDY: Christ! Mary Ann! Mary Ann! Come in here! Listen, you guys go play in the yard awhile, play on the swings. I'll call you in a little bit. (*Exit Paddy and Debbie. Enter Mommy.*)

MOMMY: What's the matter?

DADDY: Our children have absolutely no conception of reality.

MOMMY: It must be an inherited trait.

DADDY: We've been spoiling them. I think we should cut out the morning TV.

MOMMY: But I like Captain Kangaroo.

DADDY: Okay. Captain Kangaroo. But then it's *off.* Until after supper.

MOMMY: But the kids'll think they're being punished. I think you're overreacting. What brought this on anyway?

DADDY: That damn Uncle Al, I swear it's the most idiotic thing I've ever seen.

MOMMY: You shouldn't try to watch it; it's pitched below your age group, honey.

DADDY: Mary Ann I am *serious.* A jerk like that is *detrimental.* The guy has a hole in his head. That somebody *pays* him to undermine the intelligence of our children is *maddening.*

MOMMY: Oh come on. He wears a straw hat and plays the accordion. How much damage can he do?

DADDY: We'll never know, because as of now he is officially off the air. And while we're at it, we might as well come down to earth on a few other backward characters.

MOMMY: Wait a minute —

DADDY: — Like Santy Claus and the Easter Bunny. I think they've had enough fantasy goody-goody—

MOMMY: —for God's sake what harm does —

DADDY: — Lemme tell you. Day after day they have clowns and cartoon, bunnies and doggies and sickening fairy queens telling them that pretty toys and presents fall out of the sky for good little kiddies and they grow up thinking all they have to do is be good and think nice thoughts and the world will be served to them on a silver platter. I think that's unfair to them. I don't think that prepares them for living in the real world. Now call them in here, please. We're going to have a short discussion.

MOMMY: On the political situation in Cuba?

DADDY: Please. I know what I'm doing. Paddy! Debbie!

MOMMY: Well I hope they enjoyed their childhoods up 'til now.

DADDY: Just back me up, okay? We'll make this as painless as possible. Paddy and Debbie, are you guys coming? (*Enter Paddy and Debbie.*)

MOMMY: Daddy and I want to have a little talk with you.

PADDY: About Uncle Al?

DEBBIE: We *know* already. He said we couldn't watch it anymore.

DADDY: You'll get over it, Debbie. It's not the end of the world. Listen now, we're going to talk about what's *real* and what's just made up to sell candy and toys to little babies. You guys aren't little babies, right? I'd say you're practically grown-up already.

MOMMY: Well, let's not get too carried away —

DADDY: —I said *practically*. No, five years old is not grown-up completely—

DEBBIE: —I'm four.

DADDY: And neither is four, but you're both old enough to know a few simple truths. As old as you guys are, I'm sure you don't believe in Santa Claus or the Easter Bunny anymore, do you?

PADDY: (*Stricken*) Well...you mean. . . .

DEBBIE: I do! I believe in them. Why?

MOMMY: If you really have to do this, be delicate, now. . . .

DADDY: Don't worry. Listen you guys, Santa Claus, the Easter Bunny, and Uncle Al are all *fakes*, understand. They never existed and they never will. They're all a bunch of made-up, unreal fantasy characters. All fakes.

MOMMY: Thank you, Mr. Delicate. (*Paddy and Debbie are stunned.*)

DADDY: If it makes you sad, I'm sorry, but you would've learned the truth eventually.

PADDY: Does that mean we don't get anymore presents?

DADDY: You'll get presents from the same place you always got them.

Not from Santa Claus, but from Grampa and Mommy and me.

MOMMY: What Daddy means is that Santa Claus and the Easter Bunny are really us, your family. Now that's not so terrible, is it? (*Paddy and Debbie are silent.*)

DADDY: Now the same goes for the Tooth Fairy—

MOMMY: Enough! It's enough. That's all for now you guys, you can go. (*Paddy and Debbie walk out like zombies.*)

SCENE 27: (*Grampa, Paddy and Debbie watching television.*)

GROWNUP PADDY: MOMMY AND DADDY BRING HOME THE BABY.

PADDY: We're watching Red Skeleton.

GRAMPA: *Skelton!* Not skeleton. Red Skelton!

VOICE OF RED SKELTON: Goodnight, and God Bless.

DEBBIE: It's over. Now what?

GROWNUP PADDY: There came a stranger into the house. (*Enter Mommy and Daddy with bundle.*)

GRAMPA: You're back.

MOMMY: Hi.

GRAMPA: How do you feel?

MOMMY: It only hurts when I laugh.

GRAMPA: How is the baby?

MOMMY: Well, she's right here. See for yourself. Take a look at little Karen, you guys. (*The bundle emits shrill cries.*)

GRAMPA: She looks like a lobster. Cute, though. For a lobster.

DADDY: Thanks, Dad.

DEBBIE: She's pretty, Mommy. I think she's pretty.

PADDY: Why is it crying?

DADDY: That's what babies *do*. Get used to it. *You* were enough of a loud-mouth yourself. When you were baptized, you know what the priest said? In the name of the Father, and of the Son, and of the Holy Spirit, shut up!

PADDY: I remember.

MOMMY: Oh you do not. You were a week old. Say goodnight to your sister Karen Marie, we're going to sleep.

PADDY: But you just got home!

MOMMY: I'm sorry, but having a baby tired me out a little bit. Goodnight sleep tight I love and I like you you're the best boy and girl in the world and what's tomorrow?

DEBBIE: Tuesday!

PADDY: Friday!

DADDY: Christ! If today's Tuesday, what is it tomorrow?

PADDY AND DEBBIE: Wednesday!

MOMMY: Hooray! (*Kisses them, and exits.*)

DADDY: Okay you guys, hit the road. (*He kisses them.*)

PADDY: When will it be able to talk?

DADDY: The baby's a *she*, not an *it*. She'll be giving interviews in the morning.

PADDY: But what do you do with it, I mean her?

DEBBIE: You *be* her brother. (*Paddy and Debbie exit. Daddy hauls out a large jar of pennies. He empties change from various receptacles, stacks it up, puts the pennies in rolls.*)

GRAMPA: Another grandchild. That makes, let's see, Kay's four, Tim's four, and your third, so — eleven. Not bad, eh?

DADDY: Is there a contest on? Yes, Dad, you've sucessfully propagated the race. Or the faith. Whatever it is.

GRAMPA: It counts for something.

DADDY: Sure! One more little soul to nurture and infect.

SCENE 28: (*Paddy, Daddy*)

GROWNUP PADDY: THE STAIRS. From behind the railing I watch Daddy come up. Will he have on his round mad face or his long happy face?

DADDY: My round face. I told you not to play near the stairs.

PADDY: Okay, Daddy.

DADDY: I don't want to have to tell you again. Understand?

PADDY: Yes. (*Exit Daddy.*) I think I can fly to the bottom.

GROWNUP PADDY: Wait, what did Daddy just say?

PADDY: I had a dream, I flew. I just. . .flew.

GROWNUP PADDY: Don't do it.

PADDY: I just havta. . .just, get up in the air.

GROWNUP PADDY: So. . .I took a deep breath and — (*Paddy jumps.*) — jumped and fell down the steps. It was loud and I was scared but I didn't get hurt. (*Daddy runs in.*)

DADDY: Dammit! Are you okay? What did I tell you? Are you okay?

PADDY: I slipped. I slipped before I could—

DADDY: —Stand up and wiggle around. Anything broken? Think what could've happened to you. Think about it!

PADDY: I think — I think I need to make some wings, maybe.

SCENE 29: (*Grownup Paddy brings on a dark box.*)

GROWNUP PADDY: THE BASEMENT. It had two sides. On one side was the big table with my Lionel Train set. Daddy built a figure eight with hills and a tunnel. He suspended my army fighter jets on thread from the the ceiling. (*Enter Paddy. He makes "train and plane" sounds, playing on the floor. Grownup Paddy sets the box on the floor opposite Paddy.*)

GROWNUP PADDY: On the other side of the steps was the dark side of the basement. (*Paddy stops playing. He notices the box.*) Daddy said not to play in the boxes over there. (*Paddy makes a move toward the box. Daddy's voice stops him.*)

VOICE OF DADDY: Stay outa that stuff — it's full of sharp things — you'll cut yourself.

GROWNUP PADDY: But I thought it was worth the risk. (*Paddy hesitates, then goes for the box.*) The first thing I found on the dark side of the basement was . . . a small, yellow, plastic gorilla. (*Paddy examines his prize, holding it up.*) It looked pretty old.

PADDY: It's made of some *old-fashioned* kind of plastic!

GROWNUP PADDY: The texture was different from my plastic army men. Somehow finer. Worn smooth by the years. Suddenly it hit me.

PADDY: This was Daddy's when he was little.

GROWNUP PADDY: I had never thought of Daddy as a boy before.

PADDY: Hey Deb! C'mere! (*Enter Debbie.*)

DEBBIE: Huh? What're you doin'?

PADDY: Shhh! Come and look at all this stuff!

DEBBIE: What is it?

PADDY: It's from a long time ago — look. (*Debbie looks in the box.*)

DEBBIE: Hey! Here's my old teddy bear I threw up on! I wondered where he went. And he doesn't smell anymore. Here, sniff.

PADDY: He does a little.

DEBBIE: Not to me. I missed him. Look at these shoes — saddle oxfords. I wore these when I was grown-up.

PADDY: You mean you're *gonna* wear 'em?

DEBBIE: No, I *used* to wear them. When I was grown up.

PADDY: Oh.

SCENE 30: (*Daddy sits alone, with a full glass of beer he doesn't touch.*)

GROWNUP PADDY: DADDY TELLS ME THE PRESIDENT IS DEAD. (*Enter Paddy.*)

PADDY: Kindergarten, whew! What a day.

DADDY: President Kennedy is dead. He was assassinated.

PADDY: Ha! . . .no, what?

DADDY: The President was shot today. He died. (*Paddy drops his coat on the floor and runs away.*)

DADDY: Dammit. What's the matter with me? I didn't think he'd take it so hard. I was already numb from it, I guess. (*Enter Mommy.*)

MOMMY: He's been crying in his bed for about three hours. I told him, Daddy isn't dead, Daddy isn't dead. Gosh. He's. . .I was afraid that somehow he thought it was you. I said everything's going to be okay. Daddy isn't dead. We still have Daddy.

SCENE 31: (*Paddy, Debbie, in their beds.*)

GROWNUP PADDY: THE DOOR FALLS DOWN. One night, somewhere between asleep and awake, I was looking at the door between our bedroom and Grampa's bedroom. The door that was not used. The door that was unhinged. The door resting precariously unhinged in its jamb. Somewhere between asleep and awake, I looked at the door between our room and Grampa's, and it fell. (*Crash. Grampa jumps out.*)

GRAMPA: SHIT!

GROWNUP PADDY: The door fell into Grampa's room and he jumped.

GRAMPA: SHIT! (*Enter Daddy.*)

DADDY: What the hell happened?

GRAMPA: SHIT!

DADDY: Dad? Are you okay? How'd that door fall down?

PADDY: I was only looking at it!

GRAMPA: SHIT!

SCENE 32: (*Paddy and Debbie*)

GROWNUP PADDY: MOMMY SERVES PADDY AND DEBBIE LUNCH
IN THEIR BEDROOM.

PADDY: We got in trouble today.

DEBBIE: It was an accident. One of our toys got broken.

PADDY: It was because we were fighting over it. One of the players from
the basketball game. The red man.

DEBBIE: But we still have the blue one.

PADDY: But it doesn't matter — you can't play with only one man.
Anyway, we made Daddy really mad. I think because we only got the
toy yesterday.

PADDY *and* DEBBIE: It was brand new.

DEBBIE: He was hollering real loud. Not at us. But we could hear him
in the kitchen. Mommy came and said we had to stay up here in our
room all day.

PADDY: It's our punishment. We can't even go downstairs for lunch.

DEBBIE: But Mommy is bringing it up. (*Enter Mommy with tray, bowls of
soup.*)

PADDY: Is Daddy still mad at us?

MOMMY: Daddy isn't really mad at you —

DEBBIE: —he was hollering!

MOMMY: Daddy is angry at your bickering. We don't want to wake up
at 6 a.m. to the sound of your fighting. We're just a little surprised at
you, that's all. We thought you were old enough to behave yourselves,
and not break your toys like little babies. Now let's eat our tomato soup.
(*All sit and balance their bowls in their laps.*)

DEBBIE: I think Daddy doesn't like us anymore.

MOMMY: Daddy loves you. But he doesn't like it when you fight.

PADDY: When it's dark outside, can we come down?

DEBBIE: Will Daddy always be mad at us?

MOMMY: Daddy isn't mad at you. He loves you.

DEBBIE: Then why can't we come downstairs?

PADDY: Because it's our punishment, dumbo!

MOMMY: Don't call your sister that.

SCENE 33: (*Daddy sits in the kitchen, face down the the table. Grownup Paddy is nearby, studying him. Enter Mommy.*)

GROWNUP PADDY: DADDY'S HANGOVER.

MOMMY: Back in the land of the living yet? (*Daddy doesn't respond.*) You scared the hell out of the kids. If you could manage to drag yourself home before five a.m., maybe they wouldn't bother you so much. (*Pause.*) Just a suggestion. You've heard it before. (*Mommy looks at Daddy, as if suddenly recognizing him for the first time. She waits. A baby cries.*) I've got things to do. Why don't you go lie down. Not upstairs. In the living room. (*Daddy slowly stands and exits. Mommy watches after him.*)

SCENE 34: (*Daddy, with telephone.*)

GROWNUP PADDY: DADDY GETS A PROMOTION.

DADDY: Hello, Modern Finance. This is Daddy speaking. May I help you?

GROWNUP PADDY: Daddy got promoted to manager of the Modern Finance in Mount Vernon, Ohio. Home of the famous actor Paul Lynde and General Curtis LeMay. So we had to move away from Grampa's house on McKinley Street. And Grampa had to move to Uncle Kay's in White Plains.

SCENE 35: (*Daddy balances a checkbook at the table. Grampa drinks tea. Paddy plays nearby.*)

GROWNUP PADDY: A FIGHT IN THE DINING ROOM.

GRAMPA: What time are the movers coming?

DADDY: Um, in a little while. . . .

GRAMPA: Before one?

DADDY: Just a minute, I'm trying to. . . .

GRAMPA: 'Scuse me.

DADDY: . . . figure this out . . . okay, what?

GRAMPA: Are they gonna get here before one?

DADDY: One-thirty, okay?

GRAMPA: Sure, it's fine with me, whenever they come. Paid by the hour, huh?

DADDY: I don't know, Dad. I'm really not sure.

GRAMPA: It's by the hour. They take their time. Overpaid.

DADDY: If it's going to bother you to watch them. . . .

GRAMPA: Ain't going to bother me, it's just. . . .

DADDY: They're professionals, they don't need you to supervise.

GRAMPA: I won't say a word to 'em. It's your money. It's my furniture, but never mind that, I've given it to you for your new home, and if you don't care about the movers scratching it up, that's fine. Just fine.

DADDY: Anything else on your mind?

GRAMPA: Nope.

DADDY: Sure?

GRAMPA: Yep. (*Pause.*)

DADDY: If you've got something to say. . . . (*Grampa is silent.*) Suit yourself. (*Pause.*) You refill all your prescriptions? I'm only asking because if you didn't, it's okay. Kay's got a doctor and a pharmacist all lined up for you in White Plains. It's convenient to the house. Even got you a membership

in the White Plains K of C. You're gonna like it up there, Dad, I prom-
ise. Now relax, okay? (*Grampa is silent a beat.*)

GRAMPA: And if I don't?

DADDY: Huh?

GRAMPA: If I don't like it. Then what?

DADDY: Huh. Well. Then you'll. . .talk to Kay, and he'll . . .shit, Dad,
give it a chance. I thought we discussed this already. Don't start with me
now.

GRAMPA: Yeah. You and Kay discussed it.

DADDY: We've been through this, Dad. Everything's up in the air in Mount
Vernon. It's a new subdivision, far from town. White Plains just makes
more sense. Relax, dammit. It's gonna be great.

GRAMPA: Yeah, great.

DADDY: It will be, Dad. You'll see.

GRAMPA: Yeah. Okay.

DADDY: Okay?

GRAMPA: Okay. . .except for one thing.

DADDY: Yeah? Yeah? What's that?

GRAMPA: Just one. . .detail.

DADDY: Christ. And that is?

GRAMPA: Forget about it. (*Daddy slams his fist on the table.*) Just nevermind.

DADDY: What the hell are you trying to do to me?

GRAMPA: Nothin'. Not a goddamn thing.

DADDY: Well you're really pissing me off.

GRAMPA: (*After a pause*) That's your problem, not mine.

DADDY: *You* are the problem. Now what the hell is it? (*Grampa sips his
tea.*) Tell me. Tell me! (*Grampa is silent.*) Dammit! (*Daddy lunges across
the table and grabs Grampa by the collar. He pulls him across the table, knocking
the cup, saucer and ashtray to the floor.*) Now tell me!

GRAMPA: I don't want to got to White Plains, or Mount Vernon, or anywhere! I don't want to move. I like it *here*, with *you*, that's all.

DADDY: I'm sorry Dad. I'm sorry.

SCENE 36: (*Grampa, Uncle Billy, Mommy, Daddy, Paddy and Debbie. Stand-ing at the curb. Grampa and Uncle Billy hug everybody, one at a time.*)

GROWNUP PADDY: WE SAY GOOD-BYE TO GRAMPA.

UNCLE BILLY: You'll all be up to visit, right?

DADDY: Count on it, soon as I can get some time off.

GROWNUP PADDY: Uncle Billy came to drive Grampa to New York. We stood at the curb in front of the house.

UNCLE BILLY: Well, we'd better—

GRAMPA: — wait a minute. (*Grampa hugs Paddy and Debbie again.*)

GROWNUP PADDY: He hugged us hard, like he was never going to see us again.

MOMMY: We love you Dad. We'll miss you. We'll visit soon.

PADDY: Good-bye Grampa. I love you. Good-bye.

DADDY: Call us along the way, okay?

UNCLE BILLY: Along the way?

DADDY: Well, call when you get to White Plains. Good-bye, Dad.

DEBBIE: I'll miss you, Grampa. I'll miss you a whole lot.

PADDY: Wait, why does he have to go? Wait, why? Don't Grampa!

DADDY: Stop it, Pat. Stop it.

PADDY: I don't want to move. I don't want Grampa to go!

MOMMY: Paddy, don't make this hurt more than it already does.

UNCLE BILLY: Take care of yourselves, Pat, Mary Ann. God bless you.

DADDY: Hey I thought you couldn't do that anymore. Take it easy, Bill. Drive careful.

GROWNUP PADDY: Grampa was dying, but nobody knew it yet. Maybe he did. We never saw him again. (*Grampa and Uncle Billy get in the car. Paddy drops face down to the ground.*)

MOMMY: What are you doing?

DEBBIE: Wish for a helicopter, Paddy, wish for a helicopter.

SCENE 37: (*Cemetery, headstones. Daddy, Mommy, Paddy, Debbie and Baby.*)

GROWNUP PADDY: IN THE CEMETERY WE CAN'T FIND GRAMPA'S GRAVE.

PADDY: It's hot. Boy, it's hot.

DADDY: No kidding.

GROWNUP PADDY: Blinding summer sunlight exploded off of the rows of shiny marble and slabs of granite.

MOMMY: Which part of the graveyard, I mean cemetery, is he in? (*Daddy is silent.*) I said—

DADDY: —Yeah.

MOMMY: You don't have any idea?

DADDY: Shit! Were you standing there when Billy gave me directions, or not?

MOMMY: You were expecting me to remember what he was saying? I told you to write it down.

DADDY: Well I thought we'd both listen and make a team effort, you know.

MOMMY: Well you should've clued me in on your team strategy, coach. I wasn't paying attention. We could ask a guard, maybe.

PADDY: Daddy, where is —

GROWNUP PADDY: —I wouldn't ask him, right now. He's trying to figure it out.

DADDY: Ask a guard what? Do you know how many William Smiths there must *be* in this place? (*Mommy is silent.*) I mean, Christ.

MOMMY: The hell with it, then.

DADDY: The light's giving me a headache.

DEBBIE: Me too.

PADDY: What's the name of this graveyard, Daddy?

DADDY: *Cemetery*. Not graveyard. And I don't know its name.

PADDY: But it said on the gates.

DADDY: I didn't notice it, goddamit. Calvary? Woodlawn? Peaceful Acres?

MOMMY: Well if we don't ask somebody, I don't see how we'll find it.

PADDY: Why didn't we come to Grampa's funeral?

MOMMY: Because it was too far away. Besides, I don't believe funerals are a place for little children. They're too sad.

DADDY: I thought he said somewhere around here...damn. Damn, damn, damn.

MOMMY: Well we get points for trying, at least.

DADDY: We'll find it. We have to. I want the kids to. . . .

MOMMY: To what? See it, his headstone? What does it mean?

DADDY: I don't know.

MOMMY: It's not him. This isn't really necessary.

DADDY: But. . . .

MOMMY: Okay, if you want to...but just don't get so upset about it.. If only there was some shade. (*They wander, bewildered, squinting. Enter Grampa.*)

GRAMPA: They never found me. Turns out, I *was* the only Bill Smith. But they didn't ask.

GROWNUP PADDY: I know. He hates to ask directions.

SCENE 38: (*Grownup Paddy sits at the kitchen table with a cup of coffee, motionless.*)

GROWNUP PADDY: DADDY SAYS HE'S SORRY AND MOMMY SAYS IT'S OVER, IN THE KITCHEN, FIVE-THIRTY A.M. (*Enter Mommy in a bathrobe with a basket of laundry to fold.*)

MOMMY: These are gonna have to last awhile. (*Enter Daddy, dishevelled. He puts some small toys on the table. Mommy and Daddy study each other. Grownup Paddy looks into his coffee.*)

MOMMY: Good morning.

DADDY: I'm sorry.

MOMMY: We've got to stop meeting like this, you know? Ha-ha. . . . (*Mommy laughs and sobs.*) I'm not going to ask you why. Coffee?

DADDY: Uh, sure.

MOMMY: But I'm curious what you imagine I'm thinking about while I wait for you to come home. What do you suppose is going through my mind?

DADDY: Well, usually I'm trying *not* to think about you. But it doesn't work. I do think of you. . . .

MOMMY: Make you feel crummy?

DADDY: If it makes you feel any better, yes, it does.

MOMMY: Good. Here's your crummy underwear. (*Throws them on the floor.*)

DADDY: Thanks. Don't know where I'd be without you.

MOMMY: You ought to. You go there often enough. Why don't you turn around and go back there, right now?

DADDY: Because this is my house. My home. My wife. My kids.

MOMMY: Well stick around and get your fill, because we're leaving in a week.

DADDY: No you're not.

MOMMY: I've decided. I had a lot of time to think it over.

DADDY: Nobody's going anywhere.

MOMMY: Johnny and Jerome—

DADDY: —Your sainted brothers! The apostles Johnny and Jerome.

MOMMY: They're coming to take us to my family's in Middletown. They're renting a U-haul for the furniture.

DADDY: I hate to tell you but you guys are stuck with me.

MOMMY: No. I prayed for you last night. After I prayed for myself.

DADDY: Christ.

MOMMY: I try and tell myself that God is testing me. I just have to be strong, and soon, things'll get better.

DADDY: I work for Modern Finance! I'm supposed to repossess a TV set on Thanksgiving Day and this poor slob throws it through the windshield of my goddamn Plymouth! Is this just a test, God? Because I had no idea this was *exam period*, God. I didn't get a chance to study up.

MOMMY: Shut up.

DADDY: There was supposed to be something else. (*Grownup Paddy examines the toys on the table.*)

GROWNUP PADDY: Once Daddy told me that Grampa stayed out all night, one night after a payday. He'd gotten sidetracked into a bar. When he came home early in the morning, his car was full of toys for Daddy.

DADDY: I'm a hard worker, and I'm smart, but it's not enough.

MOMMY: You're just a baby. You never grew up. And as long as you're drunk all the time, you never will.

DADDY: Why'd you havta call Johnny and Jerome? Why?

MOMMY: Because I'm afraid. I'm afraid!

DADDY: Our kids are smarter than theirs. You know that.

SCENE 39: (*Mommy, Paddy*)

GROWNUP PADDY: PADDY GETS SOME NEWS.

MOMMY: What's wrong?

PADDY: Jody says her aunt read in the paper that you and Daddy...that you and Daddy are getting a divorce. It's a mistake I said. Why did it say that?

MOMMY: Christ. What kind of woman tells a five year old child...Now listen. There's nothing for you to worry about. Daddy and I are just...we're only trying to...it's for us to worry about, not you...you're going to be fine. Everything is okay, but Daddy and I are simply...Christ.

SCENE 40: (*Paddy prays on his bed.*)

GROWNUP PADDY: PADDY PRAYS TO HIS PANTHEON.

PADDY: Dear God, please make Daddy and Mommy stay together. Please make them be happy again. I promise I'll never forget my prayers ever again, I promise...Dear Jesus, please make Mommy and Daddy stay together. Please don't let them get divorced, I promise I'll say my act of contrition every night...Dear Blessed Mother, please ask Jesus and God to make Mommy and Daddy stay together. Please tell Jesus and God that they have to stay together. I promise I'll say a Hail Mary every night and every morning if you'll please, please help me and ask Jesus and God...Dear Saint Patrick please talk to the Blessed Mother and Jesus and God and ask them to make Daddy and Mommy stay together...Dear President Kennedy, I hope you're there in heaven, but even if you're in purgatory please pray to Saint Patrick and the Blessed Mother and Jesus and God for me, please pray to them that Mommy and Daddy stay together.

Oh my God I am heartily sorry for having offended Thee, and I detest my sins because of thy just punishment.

SCENE 41: (*Paddy, Debbie, Mommy with baby.*)

GROWNUP PADDY: PADDY WONDERS WHERE WE ARE.

PADDY: Aunt Audrey's blue Pontiac.

GROWNUP PADDY: LAZARUS. It was spelled out in orange neon letters that turned the raindrops on the window to orange. It was a sign on top of a building, a word they said in commercials on TV. It meant the name of a store. They had puppet shows there at Christmas. It sounded like a fun place to go on a rainy night.

PADDY: It was a rainy night. We were moving. Aunt Audrey was driving because Mom didn't know how to. The windows in the back were steamy. Mom said not to write on them with your fingers but there was not much else to do.

GROWNUP PADDY: Draw something, breathe on it, and the steam covers it up again.

PADDY: Debbie was asleep on the back seat beside me. Mom had the baby on her lap. Nobody was talking.

GROWNUP PADDY: Out the window the orange letters said LAZARUS. All those buildings in the rain were Columbus. Once when Daddy was driving he said Lazarus was a man in the Bible. Daddy said Lazarus had died and Jesus brought him back to life. It was hard to understand. There was a picture somewhere. In the thick Bible with the paintings? In the catechism book? LAZARUS. A dark face wrapped in a grey sheet.

PADDY: Do people come back to life after they're dead? Was Lazarus a ghost?

GROWNUP PADDY: No. Daddy said it was different. I had to go to the bathroom. Was Columbus always rainy? The Lazarus sign was blurry and far away.

PADDY: Why did Jesus let Lazarus die in the first place? Why did they name a store after him?

MOMMY: Your Aunt Audrey doesn't know and neither do I.

GROWNUP PADDY: There were always things that the grownups couldn't talk about. LAZARUS. Then it was only an orange light, way back there. It was too far away to read anymore, but it made a funny feeling. So did the sound of windshield wipers. They made a talking sound. The same thing over and over. Maybe it was—

PADDY: (Singing) Laza-rus, Laza-rus, Laza-rus. . . .

GROWNUP PADDY: I wanted to go back to Grampa's house on McKinley Street, but Mom said:

MOMMY: Someone else is living there now.

GROWNUP PADDY: Uncle Johnny and Uncle Jerome were in the truck with the furniture. Was it more fun in the truck? Debbie was still sleeping. Aunt Audrey's hair was long and straight and dark. She held the wheel with both hands. *Daddy* used to drive one-handed. In the tunnels, sometimes he would put his head out the window and shout to make an echo. WA-HOOOOOOOO!

PADDY: Aunt Audrey just *drives*. How much longer? Where are we?

GROWNUP PADDY: It didn't matter. Something hurt. It was hard to think about. I fell asleep. I had a dream.

PADDY: We're visiting a farmhouse. It belongs to Grampa Frey. He's Mommy's father. All the kids are asleep but me.

GROWNUP PADDY: It's summer and I lie watching the night breezes billow the curtains. A strong gust puffs them apart and lifts me from the bed. I am carried silently across the room and out the window.

PADDY: Silently across the room and out the window.

GROWNUP PADDY: I am only a little afraid.

PADDY: But I like to fly. I fly like I'm sitting up in bed, through the sycamore trees in the side yard, over the driveway, in back of the house, and out to route four. I'm not afraid.

GROWNUP PADDY: The night breezes are flying me back into town.

PADDY: Back to the house on McKinley Street, back to Grampa Smith. I know he's missing me. I can see him in his armchair with an empty lap.

GROWNUP PADDY: When I woke up everyone was asleep but Aunt Audrey. She turned on the defroster and the steam on the windows dried up. There was nothing to see but the other cars. I rolled up tight and lay down beside the hump on the floor. I listened to the road. Would Grampa come back? I couldn't ask. Would Daddy? Mom had told me that they loved each other but they couldn't stay together. Underneath me the road was speeding and humming. Her high heels clicked on the sidewalk and she said they still loved each other but they made each other sad and they needed to be apart. I listened to the road and wondered where we were.

CHRIS CINQUE

Growing Up Queer
in America

PHOTO BY FRED ANDREWS

CHRIS CINQUE has been active in theater as a writer and performer for 13 years. Her playwriting credits include *White House Wives*, produced by the Illusion Theater in Minneapolis, *Toklas, MN: The Lesbian Soap Opera*, a theater serial written in collaboration with three other Twin Cities' writers and produced independently in Minneapolis; *In Search of Merrill Strange* and *The Clearinghouse* produced by the Palace Theater in Minneapolis; and *The House That Dorothy Built*. She was a performance company member at the Palace and At the Foot of the Mountain theaters for many years.

Currently, she is touring *Growing Up Queer in America*. Chris has performed this show in Boston, Los Angeles, Washington, DC, Seattle, Nashville, North Dakota, and throughout Minnesota. (The Minnesota tour was funded in part by the Minnesota Women's Fund.) In addition, she is working on a non-linear sequel called *It's Not about Dracula Anymore*. She is a core member of the Playwrights' Center in Minneapolis and twice a Center Jerome Fellow. Chris supplements her income by freelance writing.

I CHOSE DANTE'S *Divine Comedy* as my model for *Growing Up Queer in America* mostly for its form. His journey from Hell to Purgatory to Paradise parallels my own from New Jersey to Florida to the North Shore of Lake Superior. But I also chose this work because when I read the "Inferno," I was alone in my parents' mountain home and found I couldn't sleep without a rifle by the bed and big knife under the mattress. I was afraid the devils were going to take me away in the night. Living as a queer in America, I often feel this way. And so a bond was formed.

I WOULD LIKE to thank the members of my writing group, *Bertha*; Elisa River Stacy, who directed and designed *Queer*; Trudy and Jim Cinque, Marilyn Lustig, Joan Drury, The Playwrights' Center, Joan Patchen, Linda Estel, my manager; Jill Anania and Lucinda Frantz, two technical road pros; Patrick Scully and his Cabaret; and Alissa Oppenheimer, tesora mia.

This publication is dedicated to Louise Vahle, who saw the way before I was able.

> And she, know what yearning burned in me,
> spoke softly—with so rapturous a smile
> God seemed to shine forth from her ecstasy.
> "Paradiso," Canto XXVII, v. 103-105

This play was made possible in part by a grant provided by the Minnesota State Arts Board through an appropriation by the Minnesota State Legislature. The Minnesota State Arts Board received additional funds to support this activity from the National Endowment for the Arts.

— *Chris Cinque*

(Dante's voice on tape, accompanied by the "Dante Sonata" by Franz Liszt.)

> I found myself astray in a dark grove.
> Ah! What a rough and savage place it was!
> To remember it makes me wild with fear.
> E'en Death seems hardly more bitter than there.

(Music out.)

That was Dante describing Hell. But he might as well be describing New Jersey. I should know. I was born there. Hoboken, New Jersey. The Dead Land.

I'm going to tell you the story of a girl who started out Catholic and ended up queer. It's not the only story of the American Lesbian. It's just one thread in a tapestry of 500 million untold stories. I know this story.

Inferno

(*Instrumental of "White Christmas."*)

When I was three, we had a Bing Crosby Christmas. A drifting snow covered the ground. Each tiny snowflake was a tiny lantern of cold light. Our shepherd moaned softly by the radiator. On Christmas Eve, my dad called out to me

> Look! It's Santa Claus, riding away in his sled!

I raced to the window and looked wildly down the street

> Where?! Where?!

> In the sky! He's flying! Look up! Up!
> Oops. He's gone.

But I had seen him. He looked exactly like those Christmas cards we'd gotten in the mail. I saw the reindeer curved around the bowl of the deep blue sky. I saw Santa's eyes flicker like two stars and he was gone. I kept my face pressed to the cold glass, hoping he would circle the neighborhood and land in our front yard. It was wonderful seeing Santa and the reindeer flying through the sky.

(*Music out.*)

But the next year, I met the real Santa Claus.

My parents took me on a walk through the woods that year at Christmas. I'd never been in the woods before. I'd never even heard of woods. But there it was with its tall, tall pines through which the moon shone. I grasped my mother's hand. We were on our way to meet Santa Claus!

> Are we going to the North Pole?

> Not quite.

> I thought Santa lived at the North Pole with Mrs. Santa Claus.

> Usually he does. But tonight he's at a little church.

> Ohhh. Will the elves be there?

> Maybe.

> Will Rudolph be there?!

I don't know.

So we walked and we walked. Finally, we stood on a path leading to the miniature door of a miniature church: white clapboard against the white snow, a tiny black window on either side of the tiny black door. I saw an arm beckoning inside. My mother said

Go on.

My father said

He's waiting for you.

I said

Aren't you going with me?

But they smiled, shook their heads and walked away. And from inside the church I heard (*A high wheezing cough*). Then the door swung open and I was drawn inside. Narrow pews flanked the narrow aisle. At the front, sat an emaciated man in a dingy, red suit, slouched in a hardbacked chair. His stringy beard lay grey and lifeless on his sunken chest. His eyes looked like they'd been dipped in milk. He beckoned me with a corded hand that had long yellow nails.

(*Santa speaks with a raspy, New Jersey accent.*)

Come in, my child. Sit on my lap and tell me what you want. Don't be afraid. My little helper will write down everything you say, see?

I looked up and saw a tiny man dressed in green and red. He winked at me and said

Relax!

Before I could figure out what to do, the old, awful Santa Claus reached out his long, red, fur-covered bones and sat me on his lap.

I have gifts for you, gifts to protect you in a cold, angry world. But first you must answer three questions. Ready? Here's your first question. Do you love God? (*Silence.*) Do you obey your parents? (*Silence.*) Do you honor your country? (*Silence.*) Nevermind. I can see that you're a good little girl, so I'm going to give you what you deserve. And with these gifts, you'll always know where you belong. But you gotta learn your lessons of love, honor, and obedience to be worthy of these gifts. Will

you do that for a sad, old man? (*Silence.*) Alright, here's your
first gift.

And reaching into his pack, he brought out a beautiful, blue-and-gold
wrapped package. "This," I thought, "is more like it." But when I opened
the box, inside was a briar of thorns that Santa wrapped around my legs,
saying

> This will protect you until the right man comes along. Only
> he will be able to untangle it.

And he brought out a thick, dusty book.

> These are the rules you must live by. Wicked people will try
> to mislead you, but these are the true rules. Memorize their
> wisdom, live by their precepts.

And out of the mouldering bag, he pulled a great sword. Its bright blade
cut through the church gloom.

> This is the sword of righteousness with which we slay our
> enemies. Use it well.

Then he set me down and waved. I looked up and saw my parents faces
beaming in the windows. So, I hobbled towards them, laden with my
gifts. I had become a warrior, a scholar, and a virgin for my country, my
God, and my family. My mother said

> Wasn't that fun?

My father said

> Thank you, Santa!

I turned for one last look at the horrible, old man. But he was trans-
formed! Fat, red-cheeked, a luxuriant beard, his eyes sparkled. His voice
was a melody as he sang out

> Ho, ho, ho, Merry Christ-mus!

I looked down and my gifts had disappeared — the briar, the book, and
the sword.

I thought about this all the way home. Who was he? He was so scary!
But my parents weren't upset. So. I must have made him up.

But that night, as I undressed for my bath, I found a tiny hole in my
leg that the briar had made from which the blood ran and ran.

(*Scary music.*)

My mother couldn't see it. But I could.

(*Music out.*)

I remember New Jersey as a bubbling pit. Our concrete-block house, built on land that used to be a swamp, was part of that new phenomenon called The Suburbs. But every Sunday, we'd drive into the city to visit my dad's parents in Hoboken.

Hoboken is a very historical city: the home of Marlon Brando in "On the Waterfront," the birthplace of Frank Sinatra. Every week, this magnet pulled us past mountains of steaming garbage into the steaming city, while Eddie Fischer sang "Oh, My Papa" on the radio.

(*Eddie Fischer sings "Oh, My Papa."*)

A grown man singing a love song to his father. This was my first acquaintance with same-sex love and it made an impression. And every time I heard it, I felt reaffirmed in my love for my own father, this valuable man driving our borrowed car.

(*Music out.*)

My grandparents lived in a three-story walk-up that reeked of garlic, but it smelled like heaven to me, because that is where Susie Maroni lived. Ah, Susie. She always had something interesting to show me. Once it was an eagle's claw that she stole from her Cro-Magnon brother, Mario. By pulling on a tendon, the claw would clutch and release the air. I would remember this claw the very next year when I started school. Only it would be at the end of a nun's arm.

Susie was six. I thought she was wise and a little evil. One day, she sat slouched in her little kids' chair, in her dark corner of the hallway. Her eyes were hooded, her lower lip stuck out. I knew something bad was about to happen. And then she pulled down her pants and I saw everything!

I knew that "down there" was a wicked place. I expected bats to fly out from between her legs! But she had dared me to look at her, so I couldn't look away. And even though I felt an army of devils scrambling to drag me into hell, I leaned my shoulder against the stained wall and I said

So?

It was then that I learned the only lessons that Hoboken had to teach me, a young girl growing up queer in America: how to look at evil and live. How to act nonchalant in the presence of the forbidden. And most importantly, how to enjoy it.

Looking at Susie, I flushed with anxiety, the forerunner of sexual excitement. There she sat with her pouty face and her exhibited parts: defiant, frightening, seductive. I wanted to be her. Hero worship, the forerunner of the sexual act itself. I wanted to be her.

We settled down to wait to see who would crack first. I was in danger to God, because there I was looking at evil. Susie was in danger to God. But she was also in danger to her mother. Only a door kept Mrs. Maroni from seeing her daughter with her pants down in public. God was scary, but thousands of miles away in heaven. Mrs. Maroni was just as scary and in the next apartment.

Time passed. I started to sweat. Susie started to squirm. Neither one of us would give in. Then suddenly, we heard a scraping on the floor and Mrs. Maroni's terrible voice screaming

SUSIE!

My hero fell forward in her chair, whipped up her pants, hissed in my face

Yer a creep!

and slammed into her apartment.

I had won our battle of wills. I was braver than Susie, my hero. We had made a spark in the Dead Land, a little, tiny ember and I was it.

(*Pause.*)

But that only lasted a short time, because the very next year, when I started school, I met the Pale Nun.

(*The "Agnus Dei" from the "Missa Brevis in D" by Benjamin Britten plays under the next scene.*)

I was raised Catholic. I went to Catholic school. Every day everybody went to mass, all the nuns and all the students to pray for sinners and pagan babies.

One day, I was hurrying down the church aisle, late as usual. Just having started kindergarten, I didn't understand the necessity of being on time. I had almost made it to the pew I shared with my classmates, when I felt a claw grip my shoulder. The dreaded Pale Nun had struck!

My headlong plunge, stopped by the brake of her hand on my shoulder, sent me sprawling backwards. The spinning glory of the golden tabernacle embedded itself on my eyeballs. The archangels gave a hoot of triumph at the fallen sinner.

From the floor, I looked up and up and up the great length of the nun towering above me. She wore a long, black, raven's-wing habit.

White, flying wings encircled her head. Her eyes had arched brows like a falcon. Her nostrils flared in indignation as she said

> I've watched you come late every day this year. This is the last time. Now pray for God's mercy!

(*Music out.*)

I crawled into the pew, numb with humiliation. Sister Mary Agnes had stormed into my life.

She lashed out at the other kids, too, it's true. But for some reason, she attached herself to me. As a child, I had no idea why. What had I done wrong? But looking back, I think I know.

Now, not all the nuns were as mean-spirited as Sister Agnes. Some truly loved the children, the prayers, the work. Sister Leonora for one. She had a smile that lit up a room. She loved to touch and we loved being touched by her. Her hands were large and soft and, when she talked to you, she would straighten your collar or smooth your hair. You felt so warm, you wanted to climb up into her lap and never leave. Sister Leonora loved everyone. And Sister Mary Agnes loved her.

Leonora was the only one Agnes talked quietly to. Every one else she addressed like a boot-camp Marine with a hangover.

But what I wonder now is this. In the silence of her cell, did Agnes pray? Or did she dream of enfolding sweet Sister Leonora in her aching arms and kissing her tender, red lips? And did she dream of lifting the skirts of sweet Sister Leonora and running her hand up and up her leg to a different glory? And did she feel God's teeth bite that hand to the bone? And did the pain of her guilt and frustration spill out of her mouth and onto the heads of the little children?

I think so. And I think that Agnes's longing each night must be what made her so pale each morning. But the sight of my nubile, young innocence revitalized her with a surging hate. If she couldn't triumph over the weakness of her own flesh, she would triumph over mine. Because I know now that that hand clamping itself onto my shoulder had another purpose.

Sister Mary Agnes, the clairvoyant, had an uncanny fortune-telling skill. Out of all my class, she picked me out to be the dyke with the sexual future. That hand that knew no pleasure tried to squeeze all hope of pleasure out of me. But I had a friend and he showed me the way out of the clutches of Sister Mary Agnes.

Every kid has a stuffed pet that she loves. Mine was a teddy bear that I named Caspar, after the comic-book hero, Caspar the Friendly Ghost.

One Sunday night, Caspar and I were watching a stimulating episode of "Davy Crockett" on "The Wonderful World of Disney." Now, Davy lived the kind of life I wanted to live. He didn't have to dress like a convict. He got to wear buckskin and a coonskin cap. And he didn't have any nasty old nun clawing at him all the time. All he had to worry about was Mike Fink and bears.

That night, I dreamed that Caspar and I were walking through a Kentucky forest, just feeling the breeze, just listening to the birds sing, when ahhh!, we came face to face with a 10-foot bear, dressed in a black-and-white nun's habit. Sister Mary Agnes!

She growled. I stepped back. She charged. I ran for all I was worth. I heard her crashing through the undergrowth. I felt her hot, stinking breath on my neck. I tripped! She fell on top of me. Her bulk and her habit and her fur engulfed me. I tried to scream, but couldn't. I couldn't see, I couldn't breathe. I was smothering!

So I gathered up all of my strength and I heaved the terrible weight off of me. And then I heard this music.

(*Mitch Miller and the Gang sing "You are my Sunshine."*)

I looked up and I saw Sister Mary Agnes way up in the sky, her face contorted with rage. And Caspar, who was now a 100% real ghost, and all his little ghost friends were carrying her away. And they were singing their sweet song to me.

(*Music swells and out.*)

Well, Caspar and I formed an inseparable bond that night. I took him to school with me the very next day. Sister Mary Agnes saw us coming and her claw twitched involuntarily and her eyes narrowed with distaste. She tried to take Caspar away from me, so I sunk my teeth into her hand and I wouldn't let go. Even when she yelled and slapped me on the head, I wouldn't let go. Only when her blood ran into my mouth did I let her go. She clutched her wounded hand

Only God can punish such a wicked child!

The wicked child with blood in her mouth. She left me alone after that.

One very early morning, not long after my triumph over the Pale Nun, I went into my parents' bedroom and I said

Dad, there's an alligator under my bed.

He said

No, there's not.

I said

Yes, there is.

He said

Go back to bed.

I said

I can't.

He said

Please! Before I wake up.

I said

I can't. I'm scared.

He said

Your brothers are there.

I said

They're asleep.

My mother slept on. I was scared, but I wasn't that scared. The real reason I had gone into my parents' bedroom was to try and figure out who this man was who lived in my house. Gone all day, couldn't play when he was home, because he was tired or he had a headache. So I stood my ground.

Who are you, Dad?

He put his head under the pillow. I waited. Ever since Susie, I knew how to do that. He peeked out to see if I was still there. I was. He rolled closer to my mother and pretended to snore. I didn't budge. Finally, he sat up and glared at me. I glared back. Then he sighed, got out of bed, took my hand, and led me back to the room I shared with my brothers.

This proved it! My dad loved me! But then he plopped down and fell asleep. He didn't even look under the bed. I couldn't sleep. I had looked under the bed and the alligator was still there. Six feet of menace, his head moving from side to side, his eyes rolling wildly, his jaws opening and then snapping shut. What did it mean?

I didn't find out that night, but within the year, when we moved to Florida, I understood.

You see, the alligator, indigenous to the tropics, was a messenger telling us about our journey south. I had brought my dad to the 'gator so it could beam its message up into his brain.

Leave the Dead Land and head for the Sunny South.

I was engaged in early prophecy, fulfilling my role at an uncommonly early age, the role of queers since time immemorial, that of oracle and guide.

Several weeks after this incident, I had a vision. I saw a three-color picture of a cartoon sun wearing sunglasses and a big smile. Six months later, the house was sold, the car was packed, and we were on our way out of the Dead Land, into the light. We were on our way to Florida!

Dante had this to say about Florida

(*Dante's voice on tape:*)

> The Light bark of my spirit lifts her sail
> to speed her rapid course o'er better waves,
> well-pleased to leave so cruel a sea behind.
> Harken to my song of that second realm
> wherein the human heart is purged and thus
> becomes worthy to ascend to Heaven.

(*Cello solo from "Suite No. 1 in G Major" by J.S. Bach.*)

(*Blackout.*)

Purgatorio

There's a bullet being made in some factory and it's got my name on it. I know this because Mrs. Straight told me.

She was 88 when I knew her. I was nine. She was tall and lean and she caught me on the hook of her finger when I was a girl.

We had lived in the Sunny South for nearly half my life by this time. A country of endless sunshine, interrupted only by fast, violent storms. A land of sand, ancient palm trees, and subtropical insects.

My mother, a native Floridian, was determined to teach her Yankee children southern hospitality. She would say

> Mrs. Straight is a widow and needs to have children visit her. For comfort.

So, about every tenth day, my little brother and me would cross the alley to visit old lady Straight. We never got used to how tall she was, so we would enter her house crouching with shyness. She would take her dishpan hands out of her soapy sink and dry them. She was always washing her dishes, though she lived alone. Then she'd smile and point to her ladder-backed kitchen chairs. We'd climb onto their worn seats and wait politely. She'd turn to the fat refrigerator she had to bend herself in half to see into and take out a cut-glass pitcher of fresh lemonade. Then she'd open up a package of store-bought cookies and put them on a blue Delft plate. As we ate, she'd ask how school was and we'd say

> Fine.

Then one day, she told us a story. About thirty-five years before I was born, she'd been washing her dishes, when a bullet crashed through the window, whizzed by her head, and buried itself in the wall above the sink, right next to the picture of Jesus. Then with a long finger of bone, she showed us that very same hole that that bullet had made.

Well, our mouths dropped open in astonishment. That a person could be in her very own kitchen, washing her dishes at her very own sink, and that a bullet could blast through her window and shatter her peace, frightened me as absolutely as if the bullet had at that moment entered the room.

I made a pilgrimage to the sink to look at that bullet hole and there I saw chaos. Then she gave us more lemonade like nothing had happened! My little brother grinned at me over his glass. I narrowed my eyes at him.

Think of what we've been told!

But he ignored me and asked for another cookie.

All the way home, I thought about that bullet hole and I knew I would never again visit Mrs. Straight, even if she howled with loneliness. You see, the police never found out who had shot off that gun or why. It was a random act. And the way Mrs. Straight said it

Children, it was a raaan-dom act!

I tell you, whatever feelings of safety I had accumulated during my short life packed their bags and left town forever.

(*Lights dip down and up again.*)

How does a Lesbian first fall in love and live to tell about it? I don't know. I do know she has to be strong, tough, heroic. I fell in love and here I stand before you, alive and semi-well. But I was a scrawny, weak-kneed kid with dark terror in her soul. How could I qualify as a hero? That's one of the mysteries of growing up queer in America.

My first passion was for Anna Stewart, a married woman with two small children. She had a halo of blonde hair, eyes full of lost dreams, and a smile that promised she would love only you. The first time I looked at her and felt that unmistakable feeling of falling away inside myself, I knew I was in deep, deep trouble.

I experienced this fearful moment under the wooden gaze of St. Veronica in church, Easter Sunday morning, 1965. I was 15. Anna had just dipped her finger into the holy water font and as she blessed herself, she turned. Oh! Was she turning towards me on this resurrection morning?

Then she smiled. The blood drained from my face and my eyes told her that without a doubt she was looking at a girl struck through the heart with love. Her eyes widened with surprise. She looked at her husband. I looked at my shoes.

I mean, not only did I love her, a woman, married, with children, but even more horrible, she knew it! I had heard countless stories from the nuns of blasphemers struck down dead at the instant of their blasphemy. Why was I still alive? At the same moment I was longing for death, I felt charged with light and the desire to live forever. "I know it's impossible! I know it's impossible! I know it's impossible! But what if she were to love me like I love her?!"

Anyway. My parents were friends with Anna and her husband, so that day after mass, they talked. I didn't talk. I was concentrating on this new phenomenon. All my internal organs had turned to ooze standing so near my love, so I watched my feet to see if my liver and spleen would gather in puddles around them.

Then I heard my mother say

> Our daughter can baby-sit your kids, can't you, honey.

I felt Anna's eyes singeing my hair. She touched my arm with 10,000 points of fire. She said

> Tuesday at six? See you then.

On Tuesday, I started to dress at noon. I wanted to look just right for my date. And as I dressed, I tried to think: What was it that had caused me to lust after Anna Stewart? Not TV or books and certainly not anything I'd ever seen in real life. And then a light went on. It was that movie "National Velvet." That's what did it!

In this movie the young Liz Taylor is practicing for this upcoming steeplechase. Or that's what she thinks. Then she's told she can't compete in the race — she's only a girl!

Well. We see her violet eyes get black with defiance. She chops off her hair, she dirties her face, she walks with a swagger. People ask

> Who is that beautiful young man?

It's time for the race to begin. Liz Taylor, in disguise, mounts her horse. Her horse's name is Pie. Pie prances nervously at the starting gate. The gun fires and they're off!

The young Liz Taylor, unencumbered by dense bones and heavy muscles, easily leads the pack. She and Pie jump the first fence. They are beautiful. They come to the second fence. They are graceful as birds. And on and on to the treacherous, the terrible, the dangerous last jump. She soars over it and wins the race. But because she's really only a girl, she faints.

The crowd rushes to the field. The doctor breaks through the crowd, kneels by her side, and starts to unbutton what he thinks is a young man's jacket. Her secret is about to be revealed!

And that's what I wanted to have happen to me.

I imagined crossing Anna's threshold, crashing into the barrier between us, and crumbling to the floor in a love-sodden heap. She gives a little gasp — uhh! — and rushes to unbutton my jacket, to reveal my secret. And then it happens, she can't help herself. She loses her balance and falls in love with me!

I arrived at Anna's house 45 minutes early, electric with expectation. She met me at the door. She was only wearing her slip. She asked me if I would finish washing her dishes while she hemmed her skirt. I said

    Yes.

She reached for her sewing basket.

    And as she sewed and as I washed the dishes, she told me of her first love. How he had a halo of dark hair, eyes full of lost dreams, and a smile that promised he would love only her. She loved him desperately. But he lied to her and she stood in the back of the church and wept as she watched him marry someone else. My tears burst the soap bubbles as they landed in the sink. And I vowed then and there that I would replace him. I would make Anna happy at last!

    But then she said

        Of course, it would have been a disaster if I'd married him. Everything I like is different now. Clothes, furniture, color schemes.

Then she bit her thread and left the kitchen.

    My hands stopped dead in the water. Had I heard my beloved right? Color schemes? What about the golden nugget of her desire? What about the dazzling jewel of her longing? Was my beloved shallow?

    Anna left for her night out. I put the kids to bed. They screamed

    It's only six o'clock!

Then I did something I had never done before. I drank. Not just beer, not just a little wine, but everything I could find — scotch, bourbon, vodka, vermouth, Drambuie. I was desolate. Was Life a Meaningless Joke? Could Love be traded for Furniture?

    But a funny thing happened. The more I drank, the better I felt. After all, I was in love. When I heard Anna's key in the lock, I raced to meet her. She opened the door, I threw myself into her arms. She fell back, surprised. Then took one look at my face, grabbed my hand, and led me back into the house. I was so excited! Were we going to the bedroom?

    Instead I found myself in the bathroom, my head under the bathtub faucet, being blasted with cold water. This shocked me and I said

    I love you! I love you!

She turned the water on harder.

    What is your mother going to say?

I slipped away from her.

I don't care! Run away with me!

She tried to wrap me in a towel. I tried to kiss her on the mouth. She pushed me away. I tried to kiss her again. She slapped me hard on the face and she said

You can't act like that! It's not right! It's sick! It's crazy!

(*Music.*)

I left her house like a refugee leaves a country — bewildered, disillusioned, and bereft.

Mrs. Straight's finger traced a warning on her kitchen wall to all the queers in America.

Watch out. They'll shoot you down when you least expect it. Learn to duck.

This advice made such an impression on me that to this day I can be doing the most ordinary thing, when suddenly I'll hear her voice and I'll see myself mouldering in my coffin, bone hands crossed on the cave of my breastbone, the flesh falling off my face, and my teeth showing through.

I've heard it said that we should consider our own mortality. I've done more than that. I have felt the six-foot load of earth on my chest. But what does all this have to do with being queer? I never wanted to see my grave opened before it's time. But others have. I call them the undertakers.

A good queer is a dead queer. Kill the faggots. Kill the dykes. Kill, kill, kill, kill.

Let me tell you about the time the undertakers visited me and my girlfriend Mickey Fagin. But first let me tell you about Mickey.

Short, round, red-headed, a wit sharp as Spanish Bayonet and a drawl thick as pudding. We spent every minute we could together in bed. Not for sex. We were too innocent for that. But we'd do other things, like make fun of the Dalton twins or practice screaming.

Then one day, when we were both 17, Mickey rolled over on top of me and groaned. I went rigid with astonishment.

Mickey! Are you a lesbian?!

She didn't answer, she just kept moving around. And it felt good. When she was done moving around, she acted like nothing had happened and we went to the movies.

Well, I couldn't watch the movie! I started to think

> What will my father say — we just committed a mortal sin — I can't go to mass anymore — nobody will ever want to marry me!

Then Mickey looked at me and smiled and none of that stuff mattered. Before this happened, I used to wonder

> How come I never fell in love? How come I never had a boyfriend like all the other girls? All the other girls fell in love. How come I never did?

But then I realized

> This is love! I am in love with Mickey!

Still, in deference to my dad's sensibilities, I wouldn't let her kiss me and I remained passive when we did it. Which was fine, because we were happy, we were in love.

Then one day, Mickey told me about this girls' bar she'd heard about over in Tampa, called "The Captain's Arms." So that Friday, we drove fast as we could, clear across the state to the city on the bay. We pulled into this Sinclair station and asked the attendant where Bass Street was. He said

> Bass Street. Bass Street. Oh no. Ya'll young ladies don't want to go down thataways. The only ones live down there is water rats.

We got directions from him anyway.

It was dead dark by the time we got down to the bay. The cobblestone streets were flanked by crumbling warehouses. We didn't see too many rats, but we could smell a hundred years of dead fish. Suddenly a man appeared, all long hair and torn clothes and burning eyes. He tried to flag us down. We swerved around him. We'd been warned.

Then we saw three women heading our way. We stopped. They turned a corner. We followed. They came to one of the old, raggedy, boarded-up buildings. Someone had spray-painted "Fuck you, Death" on the front. That's how they knew where to go. One of them rang a bell, a buzzer sounded, the door swung open, and they disappeared inside. Mickey and I looked at each other and we headed for that door.

I rang the bell, the buzzer sounded, and we found ourselves in a tiny entryway. A woman sat behind a thick pane of glass reading "Movie Screen" magazine and wearing a gambler's eyeshade.

Yeah?

Is this "The Captain's Arms?"

Yeah.

Can we go in?

Yeah.

Where's the door?

Where's your cards?

Huh?

You got to have memberships.

Oh.

Five bucks each.

Oh. Hahahaha. No problem.

Another buzzer sounded, another door opened, and I heard Dante say

(*Dante speaks on tape.*)

> No gloom of Hell nor deepest dark
> that may be drawn by clouds, ever
> drew such a veil across my face as
> did the smoke that wrapped us in
> that place. The sting was more than
> open eyes could stand. My wise and
> faithful friend drew near me and let
> me grasp her shoulder with my hand.

(*Red light drenches the stage. We are nearly deafened by the Supremes singing "There's No Stopping Us Now." After the first verse, the music softens to background volume.*)

Shadows sat at black tables encircling the dance floor. Black figures swung by as we made our way to the bar with as much poise as we could manage. The bartender was the largest woman I had ever seen. She wore a yachting cap and sunglasses. She had huge ships tattooed on both her arms. I figured

That's the captain and those are her arms.

We drank our beer without taking a breath. Then we danced. And we drank and we danced and we danced and we drank and we had a wonderful time!

(*Music up loud and then soft again.*)

There was this one couple jitterbugging like I'd never seen. One of them had slicked-back hair and she smoked while they danced. Her girlfriend was tall in her beehive and high heels. They twirled and dipped and swayed and made that smokey room glow.

Then Mickey and I held each other close. And I let her kiss me for the first time. It was so wonderful! We were surrounded by women like ourselves! We were having a party in Purgatory!

(*Music up, then down.*)

Then the buzzer sounded twice and the captain called out

Vice!

(*Music out abruptly.*)

Everyone split apart and went back to their tables. Except for Mickey and me. The woman with the beehive separated us and said

Wait 'til they're gone.

In walked three men in suits. The undertakers had arrived. Their shoes shone like bullets, their faces carried identical smirks. They stood in the middle of the dance floor, but they hadn't come to dance. Three pairs of eyes like laser beams peered into the shadows. They took their time looking over that crowd. Most of the women looked at the ceiling or the floor. A couple of the women looked right at the men. But nobody moved, nobody spoke, and nobody touched anybody else. The speakers hummed, the smoke hung like sheets in the still air. A woman coughed softly. One of the men said

O.K. Let's get out of this pisshole.

Then they strolled out of the bar and slammed the door behind them.

(*Elvis sings "Jailhouse Rock."*)

Everybody started talking, laughing, and dancing again. I asked a small woman with a pipe

Can you tell me what just happened?

Relax. They won't be back again tonight.

What were they doing?

They're vice cops. If they'd seen you touching your girlfriend here, they would have arrested you.

Just like that?

Just like that.

They can't do that.

Wanna bet?

I mean, they can't just come in here like that.

Hey, they just did.

The cops didn't flash their guns. They didn't even unbutton their jackets. But I felt the bullets zing by our heads and remembering the words of Mrs. Straight, we ducked on out of there and headed on home.

(*Blackout.*)

Paradiso

Mickey and I split up when we finished college. We had to. We thought we were each others enemies. Someone had tricked us into thinking that. Now, who do you suppose that was? God? The President? My Dad? It's one of the big secrets of growing up queer in America. Everything is such a big, fucking secret about being queer in this mean, fucking country. And Mickey and I got so confused about who we were and about what we felt about each other that we couldn't see the real enemy crouched outside our door. So we turned against each other. We turned on each other. It got so bad between us that eventually we realized we had to say goodbye. So we said goodbye and that was that. I headed west for the Mississippi and Mickey stayed behind in Florida. It hurt as much to leave as it would have hurt to stay.

I ended up on the North Shore of Lake Superior. I found myself a cabin in the woods and a job in a sawmill. I worked with grey shadows and I was like a shadow. But there was this one woman I had to armor myself against. Her name was Julia and she had eyes like blue beams of light. But I had had enough of love and its promises of paradise. I wanted to be solitary, eccentric, celibate, like those old crazy people you hear about. Yeah, my life suited me just fine. My house was tight and cozy, my job was full of screaming saws and flying wood. And my co-workers left me alone in a way unknown to a Southerner. These people had no gift for hospitality. I began to forget who I was, what I had been. I found this emptiness peaceful.

But I did fall in love — with the lake and her twelve shades of blue. My house was on a ridge and every morning I'd go out into the yard and look down at the great lake. In summer I'd go out naked. In winter, I'd wear boots. The sight made me feel welcomed into the world each day and if the fog was too thick to see, I'd still know she was there. Then I'd go to work. So the time passed.

I took great comfort in my solitude. But sometimes I would get wild with loneliness and I'd remember Mrs. Straight howling in her kitchen. On one of those days at the grocery store, I saw three women buying more food than three women would ever eat. I'd seen them before. I'd figured they were dykes, so of course, I avoided them. But that day, when they drove off, I loaded my groceries into my car and I followed.

They went way back up into the woods. Finally, they pulled into this clearing. There were cars parked all over the place. I drove on past, stopped, and walked back. I wanted to see, but not be seen, so I hid in the woods.

It was dusk. A woman was lighting candles in white paper bags. These lanterns made the shadows dance. There were more women there than I'd ever seen before in one place. Several of them sat leaning easily against each other. I listened to the murmuring of their voices and their laughter, the sound of the dogs running through the grass, and it was all so peaceful, I fell asleep.

(*Music: "Communitizing" by Larkin.*)

When I woke up, the northern lights were flashing messages in the sky, great green and blue and white words that flowed into each other before I could decipher them. Then I heard music which seemed to come from these lights, until I realized it was the women gathered around the fire who were making the sound. One of them stood up. She had wild, white hair and talked with her hands while another woman translated. This is what she said.

(*The actor simultaneously speaks and signs the following lines.*)

> Once, when I was a child, I looked out of a window and I felt the joy of heaven promised by the priests. I thought "I want to be worthy of that heaven, so I'll wait and obey all the laws." And I did just that, through all the long, sad days of childhood and into my womanhood. But that glorious feeling never once returned. I thought it was because I lacked faith, so I fasted and prayed harder. Still, I felt empty. But now I understand that that one glimpse into paradise had nothing to do with the religion of my fathers. I realize that I had looked, not at their heaven, but at a long forgotten paradise, back past all the horrors of this age, back to the days when you and I were favored, loved, honored, happy. Our mother-god watches over us and will help us keep her flame alive until our time comes 'round again.

(*Music out.*)

I walked slowly back to my car. The ice cream I had bought at the grocery store had melted all over the back seat. I didn't care. I drove the long way home at five miles an hour thinking, "Maybe I spend too much time alone. Maybe I should see some people."

But by morning, I had changed my mind about that and decided to take a long walk alone along my favorite river.

(Music: "Hall of Stairs" by Vollenweider.)

The Temperance is a copper-colored river that roars through a crevasse left by the glacier. The water foams and pounds through caldrons made by stones, then spews out of the river's mouth and into the Great Lake.

As I stood watching this, I felt like I was being watched. I turned and saw saw a beautiful, dark-eyed woman studying me. Then she headed up-river like she expected me to follow her. I couldn't do that. Why would I?

Instead, I headed down an embankment into the birch forest that edges the river. I walked in and out of leafed sunlight. I heard the muted roar of the river, the sharp, sweet cry of birds. Then I heard a sound and saw her coming behind me. I stood in the middle of the path to ask her what it was she wanted. But as she got closer, my heart caught in my throat. She didn't look at me as she passed by, but her hand brushed mine. I felt fire shoot up my arm and heat my whole body. I had never felt such desire for anyone. So I did what I'd been taught to do. I ran away.

But I had to sit down. I was dizzy with longing and this wild perfume that was in the air. Then I heard a rustling of leaves and saw her rise up naked out of the foliage. She opened her arms to me. So I went to her.

But as I got closer, she became more evanescent and when I reached her, she was gone.

(Music out.)

I stood looking down at the place where we should be lying together — if she'd been real — and I thought again, "Maybe I spend too much time alone!"

So the next time my co-workers went drinking, I went with them. We sat on a breakwater, which is this curving concrete pier out in the lake, and drank a whole bottle of Tequila, all the way down to the worm. It was a night of deep solemnity and great hilarity, the kind that only drunks can create, but which makes a lasting impression.

Ohhh, we had a good time last night!

But nobody can remember why. But what I do remember is Julia, with her eyes like blue flames, kissing me right on the mouth. Everyone stopped talking and stared. My well-kept secret was out in the open. Everyone was looking at it. So I turned over on my belly and slid headfirst off the pier into the icy waters of Lake Superior and cracked my head what felt to be wide open. Then I lost consciousness.

(Music.)

But it seemed that I heard a voice calling me under the water. And it seemed I dove deeper to hear it. And there she was, my beautiful, dark-eyed woman. She grabbed my hand and we sped fast as light under the lake.

I saw bright scenes flash beneath us: a procession, a feast, a circus. All made up of women and glowing with bright light. Finally, we surfaced and there was this ship, so we climbed aboard. It was full of singing and moving bodies, all glowing with this light. But an even greater light encircled the bow and the greatest music came from there. This great light that all we lesser lights faced was the most beautiful thing I had ever seen. It was white and, at the same time, full of all the colors of light. It pulsated and, I don't know how light can do this, but it vibrated with good will. I felt a peacefulness I didn't know existed. Then my guide pointed to this great, circling light and she said

(*Actor speaks and signs as before.*)

> Sister, our will
> is quieted by love, that makes
> us long for what
> we have nor gives
> us thirst for more.

So I remembered the woman in the woods talking with her hands and I thought, "I'm there! Oh, Paradise!"

(*Music out.*)

Instead, I woke up on the pier, my co-workers' faces in a circle above me. Then Julia reached past all of them and pressed her head to mine and her eyes made the inside of my head feel like the light on the ship. Then she took my hand and led me away from the others. I shouldn't have looked back at them, because when I did, they all turned to salt.

Julia led me to a private place she knew of pine boughs and deep shadows. There we undressed and laid each other down. I buried my face in her large, salty breasts. She kissed me with lips so tender I forgot who I was, what I was doing. Then I remembered. My physical body! My hands, my lips, my skin. Her hands felt hot and smooth on my skin and I rose up to meet them wherever they were, until I felt all of my pulses explode.

Then she rolled on top of me with her legs open over mine and each time she brushed over me, I felt a new charge of light. She tensed in my arms and I rose up against her and we were like two tumbling rivers, rolling toward the greater sea. The sea the Christians call the abyss, but the Tantrics call the very vault of heaven.

She lay still, heavy and warm in my arms. I felt her heart beating on one side and mine beating on the other, so that it seemed we both had two. Then it seemed I heard Dante say to the sea we had just tumbled into

(*Dante's voice on tape.*)

> My hope is strong in you who for my salvation did endure to leave the imprint of your feet in Hell.
>
> Preserve towards me your generosity. And may this soul of mine which you have healed fly pleasing to you when freed by Death's bell.

And so, I arrived at last in Paradise.

(*Pause.*)

Now what?

TERRANCE J. LAPPIN

Hit By a Cab

TERRANCE J. LAPPIN was born in St. Paul, MN on March 20, 1949. His undergraduate work was completed at the University of Minnesota in the College of Liberal Arts, Humanities. He was in the Honors Seminar under John Berryman, professor, at the time of the poet's death. He has published one chapbook, *Off Esplanade*, in 1977. In 1976, 1977 and 1978 he wrote and produced three new plays: *Re Vera, A Change in Health,* and *Hit By a Cab* all performed in Minneapolis. He was awarded a Shubert Fellowship at Carnegie Mellon University in 1978. Returning to Minneapolis, he adapted *Re Vera* to an audio visual format and produced it in conjunction with a major locally based commercial production house creating a hybrid of an avowed artistic subject recorded by career media professionals. Mr. Lappin was a charter member of the Playwrights' Lab in 1976. He currently lives in Minneapolis.

THE ONLY PERFORMANCE of the play was in 1978 at the defunct Olympia Arts Ensemble in Minneapolis, Minnesota. I was an artist-in-residence. I am able to recall each performance with clarity. This I attribute to the craftsmanship of the actors and actress and indefatigible efforts of the set, lighting and costume designers.

The realization of the text from the point of view of the director included two non-scripted elements. The decision was made to integrate rear-projection 35 mm film (now noted in the text) which was shot and edited by Scott Thoelke, a New York based film maker. A loose score for piano and cello was mixed with the improvised playing of a saxophonist. The saxophonist, who was originally scripted, hauntingly opened each evening's performance with his 'running of scales.'

I believe that the assignment of the playwright is to create a text that is always the exactitude of the human condition, not its valuation. The foundation for creativity is certainly cross disciplinary. I agree with Diego Rivera who said of art that "the work must contain the whole substance of morality, not in content, but rather by the sheer force of its aesthetic facts." For me, art is the series of unexpected glances met by that "sheer force."

HIT BY A CAB was submitted for consideration for a Shubert Fellowship in the Drama Department at Carnegie Mellon University in 1978. I can now publicly thank that institution for being honored as the recipient of that scholarship. David Ball, Professor of Drama at Duke University, formerly a faculty member at Carnegie Mellon University, and Dr. Charles M. Nolte, Professor of Theatre Arts at the University of Minnesota, Minneapolis, were both strongly in support of that submission. Their continued interest in my work has remained critical in my subsequent pursuits.

TO THOSE WHO first met me, continued to understand me, and, luckily, perhaps, judged the wisest course between the two, I mention David Cornelius, Lauri Witzkowski, William Sexton, Gertrude Hill Ffolliott, Terence Marinan, Dixon Bond, John Richardson and Kate Dayton. Also, Pax, Dr. Veritas. R.I.P. Robert Conwell, Adieux, Christian, A sheynem dank tsu, Eden, Best, George and Barbie, and tip-toe Johnny K.

To Anne deMontfort Devitt, for all. . . .

— *Terrance J. Lappin*

ORIGINAL CAST: MR UDEY: Danny Clark; HARRY STORMS: Cliff Rakerd; GENE: Gordon Tvedt; SYLVIA: Anne Devitt; AL: Robert Conwell. Directed by John Richardson. Neon by Beth Juliar. Set by Scott Coran. Lighting design by Robert Kirkland. Assistant to the producer: Terence Marinan. Produced by Terrance J. Lappin.

THE ACTION TAKES PLACE in Mr. Udey's office and in a second building owned by Mr. Udey that is directly opposite across the street in the city of Philadelphia of 1949.

Throughout the play, in the stage directions, left and right mean stage left and stage right.

Act One

A saxophone is running scales. It is an inward sound that is, at times, a substitute for speech in its range and quiet insistence. The curtain rises.

Before us are three playing areas. Left is the office of Mr. Udey in the building that is the Starland Burlesque Theater. It is usually as empty of patrons as Mr. Udey, old and dying, is of friendship. Publicity photographs of burlesque stars from four decades hang on the walls. There is a large chair that faces the window to the street. Right is the building directly opposite the burlesque theater. The forward part is a small diner that is closed. Above the diner is a small room used over the years by Mr. Udey to keep past business records and files. There is a table and chair. Outside of the window hangs a small neon.

The entire setting is wholly transparent.

After a moment, Al moves from the window to stand before the large chair. He has stopped running scales. Mr. Udey is sleeping in the chair, but he is underneath a sheet that is draped over his entire body. Al pulls the sheet off of Mr. Udey.

Mr. Udey slowly awakes. He had a mild fever from a tattoo that has become infected. He picks up his newspaper again. Taking the scissors, he begins to cut out an article.

MR. UDEY: *(As if he had read the article before he fell asleep.)* Another 16 in the New Hebrides.

A cab horn blasts.

AL: No.

MR. UDEY: The Aleutian Islands — *(A cab horn blasts.)* Too cold, too. . . .

AL: No. *(He resumes softly playing the scales.)*

Film Clip: Gene is on the street and is standing before the door to the burlesque theater. He has picked up a packet that is wrapped in brown paper. He studies it. After a moment, he removes a small knife from his pocket. He cuts the string

*from the package. Harry Storms is watching Gene's actions from a vantage point
farther away.*

MR. UDEY: Yes, too cold, too long. Like poor, red-faced Harry—

Film Clip: Harry Storms shouts at Gene "Hey."

AL: (*He has heard Harry Storms' shout and stops the scales.*) 5 to 1. Harry
pays double for any English.

*Film Clip: Gene, with the photographs, crosses the street to the entrance of the
second building. He enters the building and walks through the diner and upstairs
to the small room. He walks into the bathroom.*

HARRY STORMS: (*The young burlesque comic enters from up stage.*) Hey.

MR. UDEY: Al, you should read more —

AL: Japanese.

HARRY STORMS: The New Hebrides. . . . Hey, it was —

*Gene, a drifter and the same age as Harry Storms, enters from the right from
the bathroom. He moves to the window. He sometimes only gazes at the end
of his cigarette. Other times, he looks unsure of himself.*

GENE: So. . . so what.

HARRY STORMS: Hey, it —(*A slight pause.*) Gene? Jesus! It was hot!

GENE: So, get out—(*He drops the cigarette into a bottle that rests on the ledge
of the window.*)

AL: Aleutians. One more week with the—(*He resumes softly playing the
scales.*)

GENE: Into the jungle of the New Hebrides. (*After a moment, Gene begins
to randomly look at old receipts in the boxes.*) Green, enameled freezer. The
Hudmore Boat Company. An April mortgage. (*He looks at some more
receipts.*) A tour. East pricks west. Stan sucked oranges. Away from the
state of Rhode Island. . . .

HARRY STORMS: Hey.

Harry Storms is standing on the sidewalk before the door to the burlesque theater.

GENE: He bought oranges.

HARRY STORMS: (*A cab blasts.*) Jerk.

GENE: He took oranges in the excited state of—

HARRY STORMS: Jerk!

GENE: In Oregon. (*A slight pause. Gene again begins to randomly read receipts.*) Dye. Ink. Other supply. (*A cab horn blasts.*) Ink. Dye. Other. Shirt. Coupon. A lipstick special. Except for colored. . . . Rush the shirt for Johnny Jones. For Johnny— (*After a moment.*) The new year.

HARRY STORMS: Hey.

GENE: When.

MR. UDEY: Al. He— (*Mr. Udey reaches inside of his shirt and draws out a compress that is soaking wet form his sweat and wet with a small amount of blood.*) Gene, he says that it needs a lotion; that it. . . .

Film Clip: Sucessive passing cabs.

GENE: (*A cab blasts.*) When is the— (*Unsure of himself.*) Hear me? (*A cab blasts.*) I— (*A cab blasts.*) Out! I want all of you out.

HARRY STORMS: Hey.

AL: (*He stops playing the scales.*) 5 to 1, Harry—

HARRY STORMS: (*He steps from the curb to pick up a ten dollar bill he sees on the street.*) Hey. Hey.

AL: No.

MR. UDEY: No. Harry would never pay—

AL: (*He resumes softly playing scales.*) No.

A cab horn blasts. It is synchronized with a cab that has stopped just inches from Harry Storms. Harry Storms jumps back onto the sidewalk.

HARRY STORMS: Jerk! Hey.

GENE: Yes. But jump little man. (*After a moment.*) Move. But jump off to where. Under the street? What. . . . Open that pant cuff? (*Harry Storms has pissed in his pants.*) Spare what dignity for this ground. Hey. It's poor for the wool.

HARRY STORMS: (*He shakes his leg.*) Jerk.

GENE: The Starland is gutting itself. It's emptying. Why not fix their eyes to the ends of long wires. And from the balcony I'll lift up their eyelids slowly. Then they can leave the body home comfortable. A big arm chair.

A big arm chair to its privacy. Not elbowing into or amiss in the stink of lavatories. No elbowing over a rough sea. Rough. . . .

HARRY STORMS: (*He crosses the street to stand before the entrance of the diner.*) Hey. (*He attempts to pull the door open. It is locked. He puts his finger to the outside buzzer.*)

GENE: (*As the buzzer sounds in the small room.*) No, just forget it.

HARRY STORMS: (*Pushing the buzzer again.*) Hey.

GENE: Just leave the —(*The room goes to black as Harry Storms has shorted it out by pushing the buzzer.*)

AL: (*He stops playing the scales.*) Shit.

MR. UDEY: Oh? Al? What.

AL: It's Gene.

MR. UDEY: And Harry?

AL: Where is —(*He resumes softly playing scales.*)

Gene finally walks down the stairway to the door where Harry Storms is waiting. Harry, meanwhile, has pulled out a cigarette. Before he can light it, Gene opens the door. Harry enters.

HARRY STORMS: Hey. (*Gene has moved away. He returns and lights the cigarette in Harry's mouth.*) Hey. Thanks, pal.

GENE: Forget it.

They both go up the stairway to the small room.

HARRY STORMS: Hey! A blown fuse. Huh. A up—I never figured Harry Storms would blow an upper fuse. (*A slight pause.*) Just that outside buzzer! A small, little bell. Blew a fuse! Hey. If I'd only walked downtown tonite. If I'd only walked to downtown. Why, I could have climbed the skyline. Jesus, just the. . . .

GENE: No. Forget it.

HARRY STORMS: The climb downtown. I never the fuck figured that —

GENE: Shut up.

HARRY STORMS: (*A cab blasts. It shakes Harry.*) Huh? Oh. Still bothers you, the—

ɢᴇɴᴇ: What.

ʜᴀʀʀʏ: The cabs.

ɢᴇɴᴇ: Nickel—

ʜᴀʀʀʏ sᴛᴏʀᴍs: Better. (*A slight pause.*) You're really moving that—

ɢᴇɴᴇ: The dime and nickel—

ʜᴀʀʀʏ sᴛᴏʀᴍs: (*After a moment.*)What? Bring me here. No, I— hey.

ɢᴇɴᴇ: You smell.

ʜᴀʀʀʏ sᴛᴏʀᴍs: (*Uncomfortable.*) Huh.

ɢᴇɴᴇ: From down there. You were almost —

ʜᴀʀʀʏ sᴛᴏʀᴍs: Yeah, the son of a, the — (*A slight pause.*) Wool.

ɢᴇɴᴇ: Almost hit by a cab.

ʜᴀʀʀʏ sᴛᴏʀᴍs: Yeah. Huh? So.

ɢᴇɴᴇ: Anyway.

ʜᴀʀʀʏ sᴛᴏʀᴍs: Anyway. So — it was hot!

ɢᴇɴᴇ: Now you're up here. Standing again. Some social function or —

ʜᴀʀʀʏ sᴛᴏʀᴍs: Huh?

ɢᴇɴᴇ: Huh. Huh!

ʜᴀʀʀʏ sᴛᴏʀᴍs: Huh? Gene. Jesus! It's been two—

ɢᴇɴᴇ: Or some convention. (*In mean tone*) You got those boat shoes, Harry. You must dance the big pavillions down near the ocean.

ʜᴀʀʀʏ sᴛᴏʀᴍs: It's hot. I tell you, the New Hebrides is —

ɢᴇɴᴇ: Or do you just pull up crab boxes, from—

ʜᴀʀʀʏ sᴛᴏʀᴍs: Huh? Crabs?

ɢᴇɴᴇ: You never let the sea breezes get your sweat. Never let it cool that dancing leg?

ʜᴀʀʀʏ sᴛᴏʀᴍs: Hot. It's so—(*After a moment.*) Things could always get better. Things — A drink up here? Up here in all this. . . .

ɢᴇɴᴇ: What! Want my eyes. (*Quieter*) I mean just look around.

HARRY STORMS: Anywhere. (*After a moment.*) I will. Dye. Ink. Other. (*He begins to look through the boxes cautiously.*) Receipts. (*He sees the bottle that is on the ledge of the window.*) Drinking—(*He takes a step towards the bottle.*) Asshole is smoking again. Johnny Jones. Johnny — Two shirts for the spent gent from — Two shirts. Your winter coat, ain't it?

GENE: So. So what.

HARRY STORMS: It was — nothing.

GENE: Gambling much?

HARRY STORMS: (*Picking up the bottle from the ledge of the window.*) Huh? Sure. A Viceroy.

GENE: Chesterfields. (*He offers a cigarette to Harry.*)

HARRY STORMS: Hey. Thanks.

GENE: Gambling?

HARRY STORMS: Here? In Philadelphia? (*A slight pause.*) You mean in public.

GENE: The public.

HARRY STORMS: Huh?

The small neon outside of the window has continued to be on.

GENE: (*Looking at the neon.*) A public.

HARRY STORMS: Huh? What's it — Bird crap. (*Harry laughs.*) What's it. Bird crap. Crap. So. Hey. I — (*A cab horn blasts.*) I told you that —

GENE: What.

HARRY STORMS: (*A cab horn blasts.*) Hey. I said that—

GENE: A public that—

HARRY STORMS: Said—

GENE: Drunk—

HARRY STORMS: The leg. It draws all the—

GENE: It's one convulsion.

HARRY STORMS: All the cabs. Gene. It's the leg. You— (*Harry picks up from the table a box with some glassware inside.*) The glass. Hey. A big, fat man squeezes out of the cab. I come by. Open his door and then— (*He makes the violent motion of slamming a cab door.*) Smack. His eye...the eye glasses are falling apart, rolling. ...

GENE: The bird crap.

HARRY STORMS: Glass. ...

GENE: All the crap.

HARRY STORMS: Now jostling in some whore's bag. Glass.

GENE: I'm here.

HARRY STORMS: Yes!

GENE: (*He knocks the box from Harry's hands to the floor.*) No!

HARRY STORMS: All the cabs. So what. The cabs move. It carries a public. And....And maybe a fat, big man squeezes out of the cab and then—

GENE: I can't.

HARRY STORMS: Look at yourself, Gene. You're falling apart in your art.

AL: (*The neon goes out. He stops playing the scales.*) Shit. The neon.

MR. UDEY: Leave it hang out over the street.

HARRY STORMS: This tattoo business of yours, Gene, just piss on it. (*A cab blasts.*) Slack mouths. The cab drivers always come. Cab drivers. Foot to the floorboards. Hey. Cab driver. To the Starland Theater. Hey. Cab-by! The diner. Cabby, hey. Up here. Bring me up to the—

GENE: What's across the street.

HARRY STORMS: (*Confused*) Theater.

GENE: Huh?

HARRY STORMS: The Starland.

GENE: So.

HARRY STORMS: The big dance theater.

GENE: What.

HARRY STORMS: (*With pride*) Burlesque. ...

GENE: It's the wool.

HARRY STORMS: Theater.

GENE: What could you care.

HARRY STORMS: Care?

GENE: You. (*After a moment.*) Who are you but—

HARRY STORMS: Hey, I'm—

GENE: The appliance salesman.

HARRY STORMS: No.

GENE: Nothing. Like a standing and abandoned building.

HARRY STORMS: Sure. (*Defensively*) I got some room available.

GENE: What.

HARRY STORMS: I sell nothing.

GENE: Wallet. Huh, ten bucks? Six. Three. You're empty! You're the stump of a dream.

HARRY STORMS: (*Enraged, he hits Gene squarely in the stomach.*) No! Things will get—(*After a moment.*) Things. . . .Just piss on it.

GENE: Sure.

HARRY STORMS: Hey. Cab driver. Cabby! I'm lonely. (*Eagerly*) Got a blond!

GENE: Blond.

HARRY STORMS: Yeah, a blond.

GENE: Why not a Cadillac?

HARRY STORMS: A blond. Maybe a brunette.

GENE: Two.

HARRY STORMS: Are you crazy?

GENE: Crazy.

HARRY STORMS: Yeah. Insane. Pull it over, pul. . . .

GENE: Insane.

HARRY STORMS: A blond or maybe a brunette. The Cadillac. That's all. Piss on it. Pull over. But —(*He looks at the envelope that contains the photographs for the first time that is on the table. He does not pick it up.*) Hey. Which.

GENE: I think it's the wool.

Al and Mr. Udey exit to street level. After a few minutes, Mr. Udey tucks a bill into the pocket of Al.

MR. UDEY: You should read more.

AL: Japanese?

Al exits. Mr. Udey crosses the street. He lets himself in with his own key. He walks to the fuse box. After a moment, the lights in the small room come on again.

HARRY STORMS: Blond or maybe a brunette.

MR. UDEY: (*Entering the small room quietly.*) Any room available?

HARRY STORMS: (*He does not notice Mr. Udey.*) A brunette maybe—

MR. UDEY: Why. An idealist?

GENE: (*Not surprised by the appearance of Mr. Udey.*) You still got those boat shoes, Harry. Why didn't you remember?

MR. UDEY: Yet, I wonder. I wonder with you. Its greatest stand is where?

HARRY STORMS: (*Turning to face Mr. Udey.*) Huh?

MR. UDEY: Exactly where?

HARRY STORMS: Who writes you.

MR. UDEY: Scripts?

HARRY STORMS: Yeah.

MR. UDEY: Nobody. I overhear other—

HARRY STORMS: You should get to know Gene. He overlooks.

MR. UDEY: I overlook nobody.

HARRY STORMS: And you meet the public.

MR. UDEY: And it is my only occupation— (*Gene hurrys past him and exits into the bathroom. After a moment, he is heard wretching.*) Gene is in some—

HARRY STORMS: Huh? (*A slight pause.*) Still keep that saxophonist. That saxophonist, Al.

MR. UDEY: Al.

HARRY STORMS: That saxophonist. I see the cabs still come up to the curb.

The public is still getting out. I watch people pouring their money into
— Mr. Udey, if—

MR UDEY: (*Hardly interested in Harry.*) Yes.

HARRY STORMS: If I threw down a nickel —(*A slight pause.*) Could I even
get back a penny wish.

MR. UDEY: Gene.

The toilet flushes.

HARRY STORMS: (*Nervously*) Hey. Hey. The pavillion at the bay burned
down. Burned to the ground. I swept up the ashes of seven New York
heels. Italian? Expensive? Could be. The janitor swore he watched eight
beautiful women, but one broke her heel outside on the blocked patio.
Hey! Hey! Broke his fucking nostril with—

MR. UDEY: Today is an anniversary.

GENE: (*He returns from the bathroom.*) Huh?

HARRY STORMS: Herman? Impressed the buyer from Rhode Island. First
honest handshake he ever extended. (*With pride*) Rigor mortis. (*Expec-
ting some reaction.*) Hey. Hey.

MR. UDEY: Gene.

HARRY STORMS: What anniversary? Family?

MR. UDEY: No. (*A cab blasts.*) No. (*Gene moves blankly to the window.*) No.

HARRY STORMS: Some answer.

MR. UDEY: My—

HARRY STORMS: Some gift.

MR. UDEY: Some—

HARRY STORMS: Yeah. A blond or maybe a brunette.

MR. UDEY: (*Still looking at Gene.*) Harry. What gets your sweat.

GENE: Is she at home?

HARRY STORMS: Huh?

MR. UDEY: On the the pectoral muscle.

GENE: Harry, what gets your sweat or cools that dancing leg?

MR. UDEY: Why. Of course. (*Mr. Udey is unbuttoning his shirt in order to put his hand on that compress bandage over the tattoo.*)

HARRY STORMS: Didn't the Starland close its doors two hours ago?

MR. UDEY: (*As he takes the compress out for a moment.*) Catch it?

HARRY STORMS: And two hours later. Nothing. (*After a moment.*) And fucking—

MR. UDEY: It moved?

HARRY STORMS: Huh? What are you talking about.

MR. UDEY: Her side profile.

Gene picks up the packet of photographs from the table.

HARRY STORMS: Gene!

MR. UDEY: Take your time.

HARRY STORMS: All for five.

GENE: No. Twenty.

HARRY STORMS: Five.

MR. UDEY: Your time, Mr.—

HARRY STORMS: It's Harry—

MR. UDEY: Mr. Harry.

HARRY STORMS: Storms. Harry Storms. It never rains with Storms. (*Panicked to Gene*) Jesus.

MR. UDEY: Storms. (*Mr. Udey removes his suit jacket.*) Can you pick her out? So she is recognizable. Face her. I don't want you to leave her— (*Breaks off.*) It's the cab fare. My overhead? Across the—(*A slight pause.*) You. In fact, if I'm not careful, I may—

HARRY STORMS: I'll face her. (*Gene gives Harry the photographs.*) One beautiful. And this second. She's gorgeous. And this— (*Nobody pays any attention to him.*) Her? How tall. you know, the drop between her—

MR. UDEY: Why? What abyss.

HARRY STORMS: (*Nervously*) Huh? Hey. No, I—

MR. UDEY: What abyss. (*Weakly to Gene*) It's hot.

GENE: (*With a ball of cotton and some peroxide.*) Harry. Look along the line to the drop. Look along the line to the drop of her tit. It drops from the shoulder. It reaches down to a nipple.

HARRY STORMS: Huh? Whose nipple?

MR. UDEY: Hurry.

HARRY STORMS: No, Storms.

GENE: (*Nodding toward the photographs.*) She could model fashion with those tits.

MR. UDEY: My—

GENE: Yes.

HARRY STORMS: Yeah. (*After a moment.*) Tits.

MR. UDEY: Harry? You would miss the curve of an artichoke.

HARRY STORMS: No. (*Distracted*) I stare for hours.

MR. UDEY: Sometimes it is the entire Wednesday evening. It's her tit. It's a beauty line. The cleavage —(*A slight pause.*) Christ! It's her tit.

HARRY STORMS: And the other tit.

MR. UDEY: Closer.

HARRY STORMS: Huh?

MR. UDEY: Closer.

HARRY STORMS: (*Looks nervously at Gene.*) Yeah. (*Loudly*) No.

MR. UDEY: You can't see it. It's on a node.

GENE: The wool.

HARRY STORMS: (*Looking at Mr. Udey.*) Oh? Larger?

MR. UDEY: Bigger.

HARRY STORMS: Where.

MR. UDEY: In my left lung. (*He laughs as if he had just told a joke.*)

HARRY STORMS: Huh? I'd rather be beserk in the Starland.

MR. UDEY: Oh. Give him big breasts. Big! Here. (*He reaches inside of his pocket. He removes his hand and slowly extends it towards Harry.*) Here. Look.

HARRY STORMS: What.

MR. UDEY: Artichoke.

HARRY STORMS: Gene! The blond—(*After a moment.*) Gorgeous.

GENE: (*Begins to wipe Mr. Udey's chest.*) Crazy for her. The blond.

HARRY STORMS: Huh? Sure. Maybe the brunette. (*After a moment.*) What do I care.

MR. UDEY: Care?

HARRY STORMS: No.

MR. UDEY: (*Turning to face Harry with his chest exposed.*) Care!

HARRY STORMS: (*Horrified*) Gene!

GENE: (*A cab horn blasts.*) The arms are coming out of the worn, ragged dream to pull at the buttons of expensive shirts.

HARRY STORMS: Gene. Right now—(*Attempting some composure.*) I'll go anywhere.

GENE: The butchers are at their —Their stands and slices of evening are pared from the bones of—

HARRY STORMS: Anywhere. As long as it won't talk back. (*A slight pause.*) You're crazy. A lot crazy. In fact, piss on it, both nuts.

MR. UDEY: Hurry.

HARRY STORMS: No. It's Harry.

GENE: Who?

HARRY STORMS: Nuts.

MR. UDEY: Why?

GENE: Drunk. The drunks.

MR. UDEY: (*Grabbing the lapels of Harry Storms' jacket.*) My seed!

HARRY STORMS: Seed. (*Suddenly violently pushing Mr. Udey away.*) What seed.

MR. UDEY: Artichoke.

GENE: (*As he comes up behind Harry and pins his arms back.*) The wool!

MR. UDEY: (*Picking up the tattooing needle and turning it to 'on.'*) Your —
Your skin, Harry. Set it!

HARRY STORMS: (*Weakly*) Oh, Gene. Jesus.

Al enters from the left. He crosses the street. After a moment, he puts his hand to the buzzer. It sounds upstairs. The room goes to black.

AL: Shit.

HARRY STORMS: (*Al resumes playing the scales.*) I need a razor. I got an appointment.

MR. UDEY: You?

HARRY STORMS: Later. (*After a slight pause.*) You got a telephone.

Curtain.

Act Two

Al is standing on the street before the entrance of the burlesque theater. He is playing softly scales on the saxaphone. Gene sits alone in the small room. He looks now and then out of the window in the direction of Mr. Udey's office in the opposite building. In Mr. Udey's office, he is again sleeping in the large chair under a sheet that drapes his entire body.

AL: (*As a cab blast rips the air.*) A Cadillac. (*He resumes the scales. Gene exits.*)

Film Clip: Gene returns from the bathroom. He takes out cotton and sets it on the table. He moves to the window. Looking out he nods at Al.

AL: (*Stopping the scales.*) 5 to 1. (*Al exits by entering the door of the burlesque theater.*)

Film Clip: The interior of the office of Mr. Udey. The figure is underneath the sheet. On the walls are the photographs of past burlesque acts.

GENE: (*Entering the bathroom.*) I've been glued to that window for over one week. What do you see? Dogs following dogs. Cats. (*A slight pause.*) Cats. Woof. Woof. Bugs burrowing into the earth making great hallways of ice.

MR. UDEY: (*Entering from the hallway into his office.*) I'm hot.

GENE: There are some great men. Mr. Udey, he carries the tropics under each arm. The Amazon is a tired and old rivulet next to him.

MR. UDEY: It's hot.

GENE: His sweat—

MR. UDEY: Harry! (*He collapses.*)

GENE: The great man.

MR. UDEY: (*As he stands up slowly.*) Harry. Watch that burning cigarette.

All lights, with the exception of the neon, go to black.

GENE: You still got those boat shoes, Harry.

Film Clip: Interior of the large burlesque stage. Al is in the wings. He is talking to one of the acts, a gorgeous blond. Al "Work tonite?" Camera comes up the rows of empty seats to the solitary figure of Mr. Udey. He begins to gesticulate wildly. He is not able to be heard.

MR. UDEY: Christ. Harry!

GENE: (*As he lifts a match to his cigarette.*) The convulsion. (*A cab horn blasts.*) All the lousy dime and nickel—

MR. UDEY: Then get a flashlight. A floodlight, but I don't want—

GENE: Don't wave to me. Give no fragile trust. The wavering? It is a wavering because you always lack the backbone to—

MR. UDEY: No horsecrap! Look for the batteries then. Around here somewhere. . . .

GENE: So. (*After a slight pause.*) So what. (*A cab horn blasts.*) My life doesn't matter for anything.

MR. UDEY: No. Look somewhere. (*Heatedly*) Somewhere!

GENE: Why can't I climb the height of this shadow?

MR. UDEY: Down. Yes. Take it down. Take the— (*Pause.*) Will you set the— Set us at pre-set. (*The stage lights are set at pre-set.*) The dawn of creation! Harry! Again. Now a move to— (*The stage lights go to black again.*) Is there a question out there? (*The stage lights again come to pre-set.*) We are at half strength. Do you understand me. Harry! I said to got to — Catch up! If not, then just level it! No turns. Nothing but—

GENE: (*A cab horn blasts.*) I've—

MR. UDEY: Harry.

GENE: — heard the morning pulled screaming across the beaks of roosters.

MR. UDEY: Harry! Come on. Go!

GENE: And I hear a storm gathering of clamoring petals.

MR. UDEY: Light me up. Jesus. Harry! (*The stage lights come up.*) Yes! Bring them all up glorious.

GENE: The leper finally dances. (*A slight pause.*) It's the shake a toe-razz — razz-shake a toe-razz-razz-shake a-razz—

MR. UDEY: Now. Bring every bulb awake.

The house lights come up.

GENE: Razz-shake a toe—

MR. UDEY: It's a cross on the electrical plate for. . . .Oh, oh for — Harry!

Harry, just hold —(*A slight pause. Unsure of himself.*) Harry.

Film Clip: Gene "I'm living in dismantled day."

MR. UDEY: (*As the house lights fall to just stage lighting.*) No! Hold!

SYLVIA: (*Entering the rehearsal room.*) Can I smoke a cigarette? Or haven't you fixed the pipes? (*After a moment.*) Yeah? (*To Mr. Udey*) Thanks. Alive? Sure. No. Hardly. I came right away from the railroad station. How's Al? The two bags are at the door. Is it still raining? I'm not in a chill, I'm auditioning in a blue movie tomorrow. No cab. Nothing — Ever is? I asked the first face in the line of men oiling shoes if there was a cab to the Starland. (*Pause.*) Snap! Rub! Scrape. Huh? Snap. . . .Snap! (*Laughing*) In this city — Nothing. Nothing. All the lousy drivers. Al? Who is across the — Up there? In the window. (*To Mr. Udey quickly.*) The changes in the script. I read it on the train, but —

MR. UDEY: Changes?

SYLVIA: (*As the sound of a huge metal light stand is heard crashing to the stage floor.*) Why, in this city —(*The stage lights go to black.*) Nothing.

HARRY STORMS: (*As the stage lights come up he is standing with a grotesque rubber mask on his face.*) Change? Change? (*Laughing hysterically*) Change. Is there — (*As he looses air.*) Change. (*He faints.*)

SYLVIA: What? Laughed himself out of air.

MR. UDEY: Huh?

SYLVIA: But it can't be the first time that a comic has fallen for a laugh.

MR. UDEY: Sylvia.

SYLVIA: Yes.

MR. UDEY: Sylvia.

SYLVIA: Yes.

MR. UDEY: The rehearsal is in five minutes.

SYLVIA: He's laughed himself out of air. But it's not the first time — No. (*Hysterically*) All comics fall for a laugh. It's not the first —(*After a moment.*) Just fainted.

MR. UDEY: We'll all break for seven minutes. Questions?

SYLVIA: (*Almost mechanically*) This week do I have a dressing room?

MR. UDEY: No questions. (*After a slight pause.*) Fine. Yes, the second—Got it? So we'll all meet in one-half hour. Who — Who said that. Harry? Oh, I — (*Looking at Harry.*) Will somebody take that mask off of his face. Al? Up. Up.

SYLVIA: Will—

MR. UDEY: Mark that change.

SYLVIA: Somebody—

MR. UDEY: Up!

SYLVIA: Take—

MR. UDEY: Hard to work. I know. Is this too much horsecrap for you, Al? Is it operating? Sit down. Now, lights — Go!

SYLVIA: Run?

MR. UDEY: Cue.

SYLVIA: (*Hysterically*) Al.

MR. UDEY: Now to black! (*Stage lights go to black.*) Cue! Go! (*Stage lights come up.*)

HARRY STORMS: (*Standing on his feet and without the mask.*) Hey! (*He puts on a small hat.*) Hey! Is there ever a change? In politics? Why, I woke up to a chat with FDR more times than with a warm ass in Vermont. 1939-44. Change? No. Not in five years, but—

MR. UDEY: Oh. (*Sarcastically to Harry*) But what.

HARRY STORMS: Can't you guess?

SYLVIA: Guess.

HARRY STORMS: I am a lot more contemporary.

MR. UDEY: Harry?

HARRY STORMS: (*Eagerly*) Yes.

MR. UDEY: Will you take that hat off of your head.

HARRY STORMS: And I must be contemporary to be recognizable.

MR. UDEY: Al?

Film Clip: Harry Storms is on the stage of the burlesque theater alone. He begins to deliver his monologue.

HARRY STORMS: "Hey! Hey! Only be happy! Working! Happy! This is the opening monologue from my last hit show. It was one-half hour in running length, but you know what a matinee format will tear into. Hey! Just goes to show that — Squeeze on the orange? Yes. Juice her. Juice her. Juice her. Hey! It's just that — Hey! Does somebody have a hat? Yeah. Thank you. Where in the house did you put your ass? It was such a big house that I just played to that I auditioned for echoes just to reach the last seats. The last four rows! The final ass! Hey! This is the opening monolgue from my last hit show. The entire afternoon of entertainment."

SYLVIA: Call me a cab.

MR. UDEY: Phone.

SYLVIA: Harry?

MR. UDEY: Harry!

HARRY STORMS: Hey! Yes.

MR. UDEY: Harry, leave the boat shoes.

HARRY STORMS: Hey!

MR. UDEY: (*As he collapses again.*) I'm hot.

Film Clip: Harry Storms is at the train station in hopes of seeing Sylvia arriving in Philadelphia. To kill time, he is standing talking at the telephone. Harry: "I hate fun. 5 to 1. Thanks pal. Fucking train station. Cabby? A cab to the Starland. No, a cab from the depot to the Starland. What do you mean, jump the back of a sailor. No cabs? Tips? What do you expect. If you spit with a woman fare — Ever pull a tip from an old fare? Get it. Catch on? The make, huh? Sure. But all the vinyl is gone. Hey! Eat after work. I'll put a word in for you at the Starland. Sure. Out of town? No, you'll work here. The road is for bums. Just walk on. Get me a cab. Jerk." He hangs up the telephone. Sylvia enters the train station. Sylvia: "Harry." Harry Storms turns to her. Harry: "So. How was Boston. Train pounding?"

Curtain.

Act Three

Harry Storms and Gene are together at the diner. The stools are in pairs with one on top of the other. Harry Storms has built up his nose with a piece of actors' putty. Gene is standing near the side door.

GENE: (*Looking at the street.*) Right there. Jump the curb. Take the Cadillac over.

HARRY STORMS: (*As if the stools next to him represented a person.*) Hey. Could only be happy!

GENE: Gun her.

HARRY STORMS: Hey. Hey. I don't want to try to elbow ahead of the —

GENE: (*Watching the car move away.*) Oh.

HARRY STORMS: (*Casually plugging in an electical cord that is lying on top of the counter.*) 5 to 1. Harry pays double for any English. (*The electrical cord is the cord to the radio and the radio sound full blast. Registering a sudden shock.*) Down. Take it down.

GENE: (*Moving to the radio.*) Oh. The comic.

Gene turns the radio off. He remains behind the counter.

HARRY STORMS: Why is the world so loudly silent.

GENE: Sit down.

HARRY STORMS: Yeah. Thanks, pal.

GENE: And quiet.

HARRY STORMS: Huh?

GENE: Sit down.

HARRY STORMS: I find that—

GENE: Quiet!

HARRY STORMS: A very contemporary attitude.

GENE: Out.

HARRY STORMS: (*Reaching into his pocket for some money and motioning to all the chairs.*) Here's five. (*A slight pause.*) Don't let any of them go.

GENE: Quiet.

HARRY STORMS: I'm an —(*He takes out a second bill and sets it on top of the counter.*) Can't you guess.

GENE: No.

HARRY STORMS: An entertainer.

GENE: Oh.

HARRY STORMS: Look for the opening.

GENE: So.

HARRY STORMS: Tonite.

GENE: An actor.

HARRY STORMS: Seen one before.

GENE: You mean —(*As if unsure.*) On the street.

HARRY STORMS: Sure.

GENE: Yeah.

HARRY STORMS: (*As the insult sinks in.*) Throw that tumbler of ice.

GENE: Out.

HARRY STORMS: (*As he leaves his chair to stand at the side door.*) Al.

GENE: (*After shaking the cocktail shaker briefly.*) I don't go to the theater. (*He raises two ice cubes to his eyes.*) I like ice.

HARRY STORMS: (*Not looking at Gene.*) What?

GENE: Ice.

HARRY STORMS: Ice what. (*With a guarded excitement.*) It use to be that I could run with any idea. Ice. (*A slight pause.*) How about—

GENE: Oh.

HARRY STORMS: (*Again running jokes through his mind.*) No. Forget it.

GENE: Oh. (*Shaking the cocktail shaker.*) It's understandable. (*After a moment.*) No room.

HARRY STORMS: What kind of —

GENE: Room available?

HARRY STORMS: (*Turning into the room.*) Hey! Hey! Could only be happy! (*He strides quickly to the center of the diner.*) This is the opening monologue from my last hit show. It was one-half hour in running length, but you know what a matinee format will tear into. (*Not slowing down.*) Hey! Just goes to show that—

GENE: The comic.

HARRY STORMS: But what do I care.

GENE: Feel.

HARRY STORMS: How about "under the knife."

GENE: Under —(*A cab blasts.*)

HARRY STORMS: (*As he walks back to the side door.*) So. (*After a moment at the window.*) Why waste time with somebody hit by a cab. A hospital will—(*A cab blasts.*) It will.

GENE: (*Raising two ice cubes to his eyes from the cocktail shaker.*) I like ice.

The sound of the saxophone from offstage. After an interlude, Mr. Udey descends from the small room above the diner. He had been unconscious in the bathroom.

MR. UDEY: (*As if his eyes can't focus.*) Harry?

From the Starland, Sylvia emerges. She walks across the street to enter the diner.

SYLVIA: (*As she brushes by Harry Storms.*) Will somebody take that mask off of his face? (*To Gene*) What do you have for an upset stomach?

GENE: Cold ice.

SYLVIA: Cold? Step outside.

GENE: No. I like to see them come in. (*A slight pause.*) Ice.

SYLVIA: (*As she looks around the diner.*) It's closed.

GENE: Closed.

SYLVIA: (*Taking Harry Storms' empty glass.*) Ice.

GENE: I like ice.

SYLVIA: Water.

HARRY STORMS: (*Moving towards the diner counter.*) I—

SYLVIA: (*Sharply*) Call me a cab.

HARRY STORMS: (*Vaguely*) I did. One-half hour ago. (*A slight pause.*) I called from the corner. You know. The one over there.

SYLVIA: The corner.

MR. UDEY: (*With a surprising forcefullness.*) Yes.

SYLVIA: (*Looking at Harry Storms.*) Good.

GENE: Here's the ice water.

HARRY STORMS: (*Apathetically*) Good.

GENE: Sure. Ice.

HARRY STORMS: Hey.

SYLVIA: Please.

GENE: You know each other.

SYLVIA: Yes.

HARRY STORMS: We're entertainers.

MR. UDEY: The opening.

GENE: Tonite.

HARRY STORMS: Yeah. Tonite.

GENE: So. You know each other.

HARRY STORMS: Yeah.

SYLVIA: The same show. (*A slight pause.*) Over there. The Starland.

HARRY STORMS: The same show.

GENE: Yes.

MR. UDEY: Harry.

HARRY STORMS: Does somebody have a hat?

SYLVIA: Opening.

GENE: A show.

SYLVIA: (*As a cab horn blasts.*) The stage.

GENE: (*Picking up the cocktail shaker.*) It must be a fascinating way to put up with the public.

HARRY STORMS: (*Drawn back into the conversation.*) Huh? Yeah. Fascinating.

MR. UDEY: (*As if he regained all his vitality.*) Tremendous.

SYLVIA: If you show your tit enough, it's got to get tanned.

GENE: Your — (*Nervously to Sylvia*) Your ice water.

SYLVIA: (*To Harry Storms*) The cab?

HARRY STORMS: (*He approaches a set of the stools.*) I have. (*With great calmness*) Does somebody have a hat?

GENE: (*As he takes two ice cubes from the glass before Sylvia and raises them to his two eyes.*) I like ice.

SYLVIA: (*To Harry Storms*) Oh.

GENE: Tonite. Room available?

MR. UDEY: It's hot.

GENE: Tonite.

MR. UDEY: It's — (*Not looking at him.*) Gene.

GENE: (*Aggressively*) Tonite.

MR. UDEY: (*Not looking at Gene.*) My chest.

HARRY STORMS: (*As he begins to watch Mr. Udey.*) Jesus. (*A slight pause*) What.

MR. UDEY: It's hot.

GENE: (*Hysterically*) Tonite.

HARRY STORMS: (*Turning towards the direction of the window.*) I see a cab. Hey. Does somebody have a—

GENE: (*With determination*) Tonite.

MR. UDEY: It's—

HARRY STORMS: It's an anniversary. (*Quietly to himself*) Anniversary.

GENE: (*Moving to the side door.*) The Starland. It's beginning to swell. Oh, Harry — Harry Storms, (*Turning to Mr. Udey.*) Huh? Hey. It never rains with Storms!

MR. UDEY: (*Watching Gene.*) It's hot.

Gene has removed a packet of matches from his pocket. He makes a motion to strike one of them. The motion is slow.

HARRY STORMS: (*As a cab blasts.*) Does somebody have a hat?

MR. UDEY: (*Moves quickly to Gene and knocks the matches from Gene's hand.*)
No!

HARRY STORMS: (*Surprised*) Huh? The leper finally dances. (*A slight pause.*)
The New Hebrides. It was hot. Yeah, the comic. (*As if he was presenting
an argument.*) Missing. (*A slight pause.*) Missing. Hey. Art is a hoax. Just
juice her. Juice her. Juice—

SYLVIA: (*Not drawn into the confrontation between Mr. Udey and Gene.*) Forget
it. Harry. He's crazy. (*A slight pause.*) The cab.

GENE: I'll fix their eyes to the ends of long wires. And from the balcony,
I'll lift up their eyelids slowly.

MR UDEY: (*Weakly*) Gene. Rebuild the world.

HARRY STORMS: (*Violently drawn back into the conversation.*) I'll—

SYLVIA: Nuts.

HARRY STORMS: Bird crap.

SYLVIA: (*Agitated*) Both nuts.

HARRY STORMS: (*Evenly*) I'll tell you! Indifference is the night's trumpet,
while the sun's fanfare blows the broken reed.

SYLVIA: (*Hearing a cab horn blast.*) Harry.

HARRY STORMS: I can't go unless —(*Looks quickly at Mr. Udey.*) Unless
I have my hat. Somewhere, I'm alive—

SYLVIA: (*To herself*) Would even Christ have hung with these (*A slight
pause.*) Does somebody have a hat?

HARRY STORMS: (*Picks up two ice cubes and puts them up to his eyes.*) There.
(*A cab horn blasts.*)

*Sylvia moves over to Harry Storms. After a moment, she reaches inside of his
jacket to take out some money for the cab.*

SYLVIA: The cab. (*She attempts to put the surplus back inside of Harry Storms'
inside pocket.*)

HARRY STORMS: (*Aware of her effort.*) So. So what. (*A slight pause.*) Leave
it for the ice.

SYLVIA: Harry. The cab.

HARRY STORMS: (*Looking through the ice.*) Artichoke. Larger. It's bigger. (*A cab horn blasts.*) Hey. Don't get hit by a cab.

SYLVIA: Hurry.

HARRY STORMS: No, Harry. Harry Storms.

GENE: (*Looking blank as Mr. Udey begins to collapse into his arms.*) Woof. Woof.

MR. UDEY: (*With a superior tone to Harry Storms*) Shit. She could model fashion with that tit.

HARRY STORMS: (*Looking through the ice.*) Tits. (*A slight pause.*) No, tits.

The curtain falls.

The Playwrights' Center fuels the contemporary theater by supporting the growth, development and appreciation of the playwright and playwriting.

The Center was founded in 1971 by playwrights Eric Brogger, Tom Dunn, Barbara Field and John Jackoway. Today its programs serve approximately 350 playwrights nationwide.

Of these, 50 core members receive a range of residencies, readings and workshops each year with professional actors, directors and dramaturgs. These creative collaborations offer them the invaluable opportunity to hear, see and refine their work in a supportive environment. These activities include the Center's annual Midwest PlayLabs, an intensive two week developmental workshop each August for the work of four to six playwrights from around the country, as well as the Center's Jerome and McKnight Fellowships.

Other Playwrights' Center programs serve and educate the general public; these include an ongoing shedule of classes, a public Monday Night Reading series that tests core members' works-in-progress, a "Shoptalk" discussion series, "Storytalers," which tours members' plays to schools and community centers, Playwright-in-the-School residencies, and the Young Playwrights Summer Conference.

For more information about the Playwrights' Center, telephone or write: The Playwrights' Center, 2301 Franklin Avenue East, Minneapolis, MN 55406, tel. (612) 332-7481.